Helping Your College Student Succeed

THE PARENT's CRASH COURSE IN CAREER PLANNING

Marcia B. Harris & Sharon L. Jones

Printed on recyclable paper

 VGM Career Horizons
a division of *NTC Publishing Group*
Lincolnwood, Illinois USA

Library of Congress Cataloging-in-Publication Data

Harris, Marcia B.
     The parent's crash course in career planning : helping your
college student succeed / Marcia B. Harris, Sharon L. Jones.
          p.   cm.
     Includes bibliographical references.
     ISBN 0-8442-4491-0
     1. Vocational guidance—United States.   2. College graduates—
Employment—United States.   3. College majors—United States.
I. Jones, Sharon L. (Sharon Lynn), 1952–   .   II. Title.
HF5382.5.U5H356   1996
650.14—dc20   96-467
                                                                           CIP

Published by VGM Career Horizons, a division of NTC Publishing Group
4255 West Touhy Avenue
Lincolnwood (Chicago), Illinois 60646-1975, U.S.A.
© 1996 by NTC Publishing Group. All rights reserved.
No part of this book may be reproduced, stored in a retrieval
system, or transmitted in any form or by any means,
electronic, mechanical, photocopying, recording or otherwise,
without the prior permission of NTC Publishing Group.
Manufactured in the United States of America.

67 8 9 0 VP 9 8 7 6 5 4 3 2 1

CONTENTS

About the Authors

Marcia B. Harris is a recognized authority in the field of college career services with twenty years of experience at three different colleges and universities and additional work experience in the advertising and insurance industries. She is currently director of University Career Services at the University of North Carolina at Chapel Hill. She is the author of several journal articles and has been a consultant on college career issues for more than 25 organizations, including IBM, Philip Morris, and the FBI. Ms. Harris has served as president of the Southeastern Association of Colleges and Employers and is the recipient of several prestigious awards in the career services field, including the National Association of Colleges and Employers' Outstanding Achievement Award for Innovation. She holds a bachelor's degree from Vassar College and a master's degree from North Carolina State University. Ms. Harris is the mother of two successfully employed college graduates.

Sharon L. Jones has nineteen years of career counseling or human resources experience in university, corporate, and military settings. As associate director of University Career Services at the University of North Carolina at Chapel Hill, she has counseled students for more than ten years. She has published articles and has done public speaking on career topics. Ms. Jones worked in human resources for Exxon Office Systems Company and Mobil Oil Corporation, and has recruited on college campuses. Ms. Jones earned an associate's degree from Cottey College, a bachelor's degree from Southern Colorado State College, and a master of science degree in industrial relations from the Krannert Graduate School of Management at Purdue University. A former Army officer, she was awarded the Army Commendation Medal on active duty in Heidelberg, Germany. She also served as a captain in Army Reserve infantry and armored cavalry training battalions.

Foreword

This book has been written in response to the increasing interest among parents in helping their college-age children plan for their career. Many of today's parents realize that the job market has changed significantly from when they entered the work force, and they feel ill-prepared to advise their children.

As career counselors we have seen a steady growth in the number of inquiries we receive each year from parents of college students and of prospective students. They ask such questions as, "What is the best major?" "How many students find jobs after graduation?" and "What is the average starting salary of new graduates?"

While these questions are understandably on parents' minds, more appropriate questions would be, "How can my son or daughter receive help choosing the best major for his or her interests and abilities?" "What percentage of students majoring in _____ [marine science, history, etc.] is employed by graduation?" and "What is the average starting salary of new graduates entering the field of _____ [broadcasting, banking, etc.]?"

There are many additional, perhaps even more important, questions that parents should be asking, like, "Which skills are most in demand by employers?" "How can my son or daughter prepare while in college to be competitive in the marketplace upon graduation?" "Which services does the university provide to help my child plan for his or her career?" "When should these services be used?" and "Is graduate school necessary to enter the field in which my child is interested?"

A Parent's Crash Course in Career Planning answers these questions and many more. We hope that you will read it, discuss the contents with your college student both before and during college, and refer to it often.

We are firm believers that the advice within this book works; we have seen evidence of its success time and time again. We wish you and your child wonderful years of excitement, discovery, and growth during the college experience, and we wish your child satisfying employment upon graduation.

Acknowledgments

We wish to thank Joan Busko, Leonard Harris, Marguerite Horton, Marilyn Link, Myron Liptzin, Clay Swenson, and Judith Tawil for their many helpful suggestions and Garry Jones for his technical support.

Thanks also to Sarah Kennedy, who first saw potential in this book, and to our editor, Betsy Lancefield, for her counsel and support.

Dedication

To my husband, Lenny, for his constant love and support, and to my children, Todd and Stacey, for proving that the advice of this book works.

MBH

To my husband, Garry, for the inspiration to write this book, and to my parents, Lowell and Thelma Wiatt, for their love and encouragement.

SLJ

CHAPTER 1

GETTING A HEAD START: WHAT TO DO IN THE EARLY COLLEGE YEARS

"I'm Keeping My Options Open"

Boomerang kids. That's the term used to describe college students who are sent off to school and four or five years later are right back home, living in their old bedroom, supported by their parents. Of course, by that time the parents have turned the bedroom into an exercise or sewing room and have adjusted to their own new, independent lifestyle. They aren't real thrilled about having a boarder—especially one who doesn't pay! But what are they to do? Their child needs help, and they're going to give it.

Why is it that some students graduate from college with a job in hand—maybe having had two or three offers to choose from—whereas others spend months after graduation searching for employment and then have to settle for a job that doesn't even require a college degree?

Sometimes the answer is the particular major or career field the student has selected. A field in which employees are in high demand and short supply, like pharmacy, almost guarantees the new graduate employment. Most of the time, though, the difference between the student who has success in the job market and the one who has a great deal of difficulty is due to the difference in the preparation and planning the students have given to their future career while in college.

Many students enter college with some vague idea of what they might want to do when they finish. Few of these students actually enter those fields. It is common for students to change their mind—and indeed their major—several times while in school. They may take their first organic chemistry course and realize that perhaps medical school isn't for them after all! They may enroll in anthropology and suddenly become excited about a field they barely knew existed. Or they may have a summer internship in banking and become fascinated by the financial world.

There is nothing wrong with a student's being unsure about his or her career direction for the first few years of college. The problem comes when a student puts off thinking about a career, let alone planning for it, until shortly before graduation (or even after).

Usually students avoid preparing for a career out of a combination of fear and ignorance. They are unsure of what they want to do, which is frightening, and they are unaware of the importance of preparation while in college. Often they believe that focusing on a career direction will limit their options—anathema to most college kids! So they reason that by not planning for a career, they can keep themselves open to a myriad of possibilities, which they hope will be available upon graduation.

Unfortunately, their inaction has just the opposite effect. With few exceptions, students graduating with "only" a college degree—even from a "name" school and with good grades—are generally not able to compete in today's difficult job market. Students must take responsibility for their own employability and marketability. They cannot assume that the degree alone will enable them to meet their career goals; nor can they assume, especially at a large university, that someone from their institution will ensure that they are doing all that is necessary regarding career planning. College is like a large smorgasbord: one can choose mostly junk food and empty calories or select nutritious, well-balanced items that help build and maintain fitness. A student can go through the college experience opting for the easiest courses and spending free time partying and going to football games, or a student can choose intellectually challenging courses, participate in meaningful activities, and prepare for future career possibilities.

The Bureau of Labor Statistics projects that between 1992 and 2005, 17.9 million college graduates will be competing for 13.7 million jobs requiring college degrees. Because of this imbalance between the number of graduates and the number of opportunities for them, nearly one in every four new graduates will have to settle for a job that doesn't require a degree.

Employers, having such a vast supply of new graduates to choose from (almost 1.4 million a year), are becoming increasingly particular about their requirements. Whereas in the past they were primarily looking for bright, well-educated young people, today they are looking for young people who are bright and well-educated, but who also *have skills in areas of interest to them*—such as accounting or computers—*have demonstrated leadership experience*, and *have relevant work experience*.

You, as a parent, can do much to help your son or daughter acquire the credentials for entering a satisfying career. You will need the interest to become involved (you probably have that or you wouldn't be reading this book), the knowledge of how to help (we'll be giving you that), and the commitment to periodically discuss your child's future with him or her. (Occasional well-informed, well-intentioned "meddling" can be healthy!) Periodic discussions with your child about the future can not only help assure that important steps towards planning will be taken, but these discussions can also help maintain closeness while your young adult is undergoing the process of changing from college student to professional. With luck, your gentle reminders and questions will be appreciated. It is important not to overdo it, though, and to keep in mind that your son or daughter should ultimately be making the final decision about career selection and goals.

When to Do What

Freshman Year—Easing into College Life

Freshmen have a big job—that of adjusting to college. Even if your child is a good student, self-sufficient, easygoing, and friendly, this may be the first time he or she has had to move to a new city, live in one small room with a stranger, balance a checkbook, navigate an unfamiliar campus, *and* adjust to a far greater academic workload and level of competition than ever before. This is not the best time to bring up career planning! Most freshmen have so much going on in their lives that the vast majority are simply not receptive to planning far into the future.

Students should spend the first year acclimating to campus life and college-level course work. Some find the first year, particularly the first semester, quite easy academically. They are often the students who have had an excellent secondary school preparation and have entered college with advanced credit. They may even comment that their courses are "a review of high school material." These students may have great grades in their first semester despite lackadaisical study habits. They assume that subsequent semesters will be just as easy and then find to their dismay that their grades steadily slide as the courses get harder.

Other students don't know what hit them that first semester. If they haven't had a strong high school preparation or did not face much competition from their peers, they will soon find that the course work and faculty expectations about performance are far greater than they have ever had to deal with. Their grades may be abysmal the first semester, which will be discouraging to them (as well as to you). But most students, with effort and possibly academic support from their school, can recover from one bad semester—especially if it is their first one. Rarely, though, can a student who has had two years of poor grades bring them up to a competitive level by their senior year. (A competitive level would mean a grade point average—or GPA—of about 3.0 on a 4.0 scale for most career fields. But this could be significantly higher for some other fields or for graduate or professional school admission.) Good grades, especially for freshmen, require a major commitment of time and effort. A recent study of the University of Iowa found that freshmen who studied four or more hours a day had average GPAs of 3.0, while those who studied less than one hour a day averaged 2.6.

So encourage your son or daughter to make grades a top priority from the beginning. Students who start out investing the time and effort to make good grades develop habits and skills that serve them well throughout college.

Freshmen should begin establishing good relationships with their academic adviser and faculty members, especially those in fields that interest them. These individuals can provide excellent career and academic advice and can serve as references for part-time jobs, internships, and eventually full-time positions. Often faculty and advisers are eager to get to know students on an individual basis but expect the student to take the initiative by scheduling appointments or staying after class to talk.

The freshman year is also a time for students to become involved in at least one extracurricular activity. Virtually every campus has a large variety of clubs and organizations, as well as other opportunities for students to engage in activities that interest them. Does your son enjoy writing? He can volunteer to write for the campus newspaper or other campus publications. Does your daughter have in interest in computers? She can sign up for the computer science or math club. Does he like to help others? He can volunteer for the Big Buddy program. Does she want to explore business opportunities? She can join the Business Student Association. Generally there will be an activity for almost any interest a student has. And if there isn't one, the student always has the option of forming a new organization, which is usually quite easy to do. Becoming involved in campus life, whether through student government, the residence hall, the drama club, the ski team, or a fraternity or sorority, will help your child find a niche and develop a feeling of belonging. This is critical to adjustment to college and is a major factor in a student's staying in school and in being satisfied with college life.

As we will discuss later, extracurricular activities are one of the best ways to explore career interests, obtain leadership experience, and acquire skills, such as public speaking, writing, budgeting, and organizing, that are important in entering and succeeding in a career.

Students should use their summers constructively. Although it is unlikely that freshmen will be able to obtain an internship, they may be able to work in a field of interest to them, although it will probably be at a low level. If they have an interest in banking, they can work as a teller; if they want to explore retailing, they can work as a sales assistant in a department store; if they want exposure to the work of a veterinarian, they may be able to do clerical work in a veterinary clinic; if they want to work with children, they can be a summer camp counselor. Any type of hands-on experience will be helpful and good for the résumé later.

Other worthwhile summer activities for freshmen are study abroad, travel, volunteer work, and summer school (to bring up grades, take courses they may not be able to get into during the school year, or build credit hours in order to be able to take a lighter load some time in the future).

Sophomore and Junior Years—Time for Career Planning

Assuming that a student has made the transition to college life and is handling it fairly well, the sophomore year is typically the time to begin career planning.

What exactly is career planning? For college students career planning involves assessing their interests, skills, abilities, and work values; deciding, either generally or specifically, what it is they want to do in life (or at least for the first few years after college); learning about the qualifications necessary to enter their desired field; and—during the next two to three years—obtaining these qualifications as well as other "enhancers" in order to be a strong candidate to compete for positions in their chosen career.

A student who uses the sophomore and junior years wisely will be well prepared to seek an entry-level position in a rewarding career field during his or her senior year. In Chapter 8 we'll discuss senior-year job-search strategies in more depth.

Five Steps to Career Planning

1. Self-Assessment

As the first step to choosing a career, your child should assess his or her interests, skills, abilities, and work values. Every college can provide help with this process. The campus counseling center or career office offers interest and personality inventories, which can be a good starting point. Interest inventories, or "tests," such as the Campbell Interest Inventory and the Self-Directed Search, can help students assess their likes and dislikes and also measure the similarity of their likes and dislikes to those of successful workers in various occupations. (Research indicates that having similar interests to those successfully employed in a career field is likely to result in satisfaction with that field.) Personality tests, such as the Myers-Briggs Type Indicator, also provide useful data. Many career or counseling centers offer computerized guidance programs like SIGI or DISCOVER, which students enjoy taking and find helpful.

No test exists, though, that can tell your son or daughter precisely what he or she should do with his or her life. Nor are there many tests that measure aptitude—what a person is good at. (Generally grades and college entrance tests like the SAT or ACT are fairly good indicators of how strong a student is in verbal and quantitative disciplines. This information can be useful when considering careers that require rigorous academic training.)

Interest and personality inventories primarily help identify patterns of an individual's interests and suggest occupations that might fit these patterns. Through further discussions with a career counselor, your son or daughter can begin to form ideas about occupations that might suit his or her values, abilities, and interests. It is important not to overlook lifestyle and work-condition issues, which include income level, working hours, work attire, prestige of position, and work environment, among others. Although these factors should not unduly influence career choice, they certainly must be considered.

Some colleges offer a career planning course for academic credit. This type of course is especially useful for freshmen and sophomores who are unsure about their major or career. Taking a career planning course is also an excellent way to ensure that at least a minimum amount of planning for the future will be done in college, since it imposes some structure and requirements upon students who, like so many of us, may be prone to procrastination.

2. Research and Exploration

The next step involves exploring possible occupations. Unfortunately, many college students choose a major or a career direction based on very little information. For instance, law school admissions offices experienced a tremendous surge of interest in law during the popularity of the TV show "L.A. Law." Students enamored of the glamour of expensive suits, glitzy offices, and unusual law cases decided to be lawyers! But many of them sadly later learned that for most lawyers, the reality of practicing law bears little resemblance to how it is portrayed on television.

Students can explore careers that interest them in a number of ways: reading, talking to those practicing or knowledgeable about the career, and exposure to the actual working environment.

Reading and Viewing Information

It is often said that students spend more time researching the choice of a stereo than the choice of a career. Time and energy put into obtaining as much career information as possible from a variety of sources will be well worth it.

Books, professional journals, and videotapes are important and valuable sources of career information. The career offices and the campus library will have a wealth of these resources. Encourage your son or daughter to read a variety of materials to get different opinions and perspectives. *The Occupational Outlook Handbook,* published biannually by the U.S. Department of Labor, gives an overview of almost every career field a college student is likely to be considering. It also includes sources to contact for further information.

Talking to Others

Encourage your child to talk to people who are doing the kind of work that interests him or her. You may know someone working in the field or, through contacts, may be able to find someone who does. If not, have your child ask the career center or faculty members for names of alumni or other contacts. Another possibility is to look into professional associations related to the field and write for information and local contact names. Many of these associations have student chapters on campus or allow students to attend local meetings—a great way to gain information and also start developing a network of contacts. If your child has an interest in personnel work (now usually called human resources), he or she should check to see whether there is a campus student chapter of the Society for Human Resource Management. Books such as *The Occupational Outlook Handbook* or *The Encyclopedia of Associations,* available in the college library or career center, have information about relevant professional associations. Local service organizations like the Rotary Club or Civitans may also be helpful.

Students should conduct "information interviews" once they have located contacts in the fields of interest to them. Unlike a job interview, an information interview is conducted by the student (as opposed to the employer) and, as the name implies, is for informational purposes only. Most people love talking with others about what they do, and most professionals especially enjoy giving advice to students. The career center can coach your son or daughter on how to approach someone to request an information interview, how to develop a list of questions to ask, and how to actually conduct the interview. It is always important to send a thank-you letter within a week, and the smart student will stay in touch from time to time to retain the contact.

Colleges offer numerous other ways for underclassmen to begin making contacts with and learning from employers. Most schools hold career fairs and other career-related programs, such as career panels, employer presentations, and graduate/professional school days. Sophomores and juniors (and interested freshmen) should attend these programs and ask questions about entry-level requirements and desired qualifications. Students should use these events to begin getting to know employers and using them as resources. A student who has an interest in a career in consumer sales, for example, can start preparing for it by asking Procter & Gamble or General Foods recruiters at a campus career fair for advice on a major, course work, part-time or summer work experience, and extracurricular activities. Even with the hundreds—and sometimes thousands—of students these recruiters meet on the many campuses they visit, they often remember the assertive student who has talked with them each year starting as a freshman or sophomore. By the time that student is a senior and ready to seek a job, he or she is known to the recruiter and has an edge over students who are starting from scratch.

3. Gaining Experience

Since the freshman year is primarily spent adjusting to college and the senior year either looking for a job or applying to graduate school (or possibly both), a student has basically only two years to become the best possible candidate for obtaining his or her goal upon graduation. Whether that goal is an entry-level job or admission to graduate or professional school, it is essential for the student to maximize opportunities during the sophomore and junior years to acquire the credentials that will give an advantage over the many other applicants competing for the same goal.

Extracurricular Activities

We've already discussed the value of participation in extracurricular activities. Not only do these activities help students make friends and find a place of belonging, but they also provide opportunities for learning about careers and for developing and demonstrating many skills.

Almost every employer hiring new college graduates seeks students with leadership skills. How do students acquire and demonstrate leadership skills? Usually through volunteering for or being elected to positions of leadership and responsibility in student government, their sorority or fraternity, the residence hall, athletics, or campus organizations. Students may also participate in activities off-campus, such as religious, community service, or political groups. Students must bear in mind that it may take several years to grow into and earn significant leadership positions.

Some students join so many organizations that they spread themselves too thin. Their grades may suffer, and they may find themselves feeling very stressed. Generally it is advisable for a student to be involved in no more than three extracurricular activities (fewer in their first year or two), and to try to have substantial leadership roles in the activities they select.

Experience

Years ago college seniors bemoaned the catch-22 of getting experience. "Every employer," they would say, "wants to hire someone with experience. How can you ever get experience if no one will hire you without it?" Today that is not a valid complaint. There are numerous ways for students to obtain relevant work experience while still in school.

Field Experience/Cooperative Education   Students—and their parents—must realize that obtaining marketable skills and career-related experience is a critical part of their education. For some majors experience will be built into the curriculum. Education majors, for example, do student teaching, so they graduate with experience in their field. Nursing, pharmacy, and most health-related majors have "clinical rotations" in hospitals or other appropriate work settings. Many technical majors, like engineering or computer science, are either required or have the option to participate in cooperative education programs and thus have a significant amount of experience upon graduation.

You already may have heard of cooperative education but you may not be certain of its meaning. Cooperative education is an academic program that alternates periods of study on-campus with periods of career-related work experience off-campus. For example, a student studying electrical engineering may be a full-time student on campus in the fall semester, then work full-time for an employer like IBM in the spring semester (off-campus, but obtaining course credit for the work experience), and then return to campus full-time in the summer or the next fall. Generally a student involved in a cooperative education program (usually called co-op) will have two to three work experiences, often with the same employer. Co-op allows the student to test out a career, make contacts, and obtain work experience. Additionally, co-op experience almost always is paid and carries academic credit. It is an ideal way to blend academic and work experience. The only possible drawback is that it usually extends graduation to at least five years. Co-op programs are almost always available to students in technical programs like engineering and may be available to others, depending on the college or university. It may also be possible for students attending colleges without a cooperative education program to create a similar type of experience with the help of the career or internship office.

Part-Time Jobs, Volunteer Work, and Internships   Students in most majors do not have a ready-made path to obtain experience. But there are many ways for them to do so through part-time jobs, volunteer work, and internships. All else being equal, many employers favor the candidate who has held a part-time job while in school. As a recruiter from Nissan Motor states, "Working part-time—even at an unrelated job—demonstrates industriousness, organizational skills, and knowledge of the expectations of the working world."

Part-time jobs are available both on campus and with employers in college communities. Students might need to be creative in finding them, though. Encourage your child to read the classified ads in the campus and local newspaper. Both the financial aid and career offices may post part-time job listings. He or she should also directly approach campus departments, faculty members, and local employers to inquire about work. The biology or chemistry department is a natural place for a student wishing to get lab experience to look. But that same student might not think about contacting the university medical, dental, or veterinary school, local hospitals, health care clinics, pharmaceutical firms, or drug analysis companies. Likewise, in addition to the campus data processing or computer science department, a student wanting to acquire computer skills might check with the library, the accounting office, or even the career center—all of which use computers and usually need more expertise in this area.

In addition to part-time jobs, students may volunteer to work unpaid in exchange for training and experience. In some fields it is very difficult for students to find paid positions. This is especially true in the arts, broadcasting, entertainment, journalism, museum work, government and politics, anthropology, and other fields that are not in high demand. Although it may be hard for you, and your son or daughter, to accept the fact that he or she may have to work "for free," if you consider this as another part of the total educational experience, it may be easier to swallow. (At least you're not paying tuition for it!)

What exactly is an internship? The definition may differ from campus to campus, but the common thread among internships is that they are career-related learning experiences. Beyond that they may vary significantly. They may be paid or unpaid, be full-time or part-time, take place during the summer or the school year, and carry academic credit or not. More information on internships will be given in Chapter 5.

4. Developing Marketable Skills and Enhancers

Most employers today are less interested in a student's major than in the student's skills. A prominent management consultant was recently quoted in *Fortune* magazine as saying, "Special skills and abilities have moved from being the way to win to being the price of admission."

Although some fields, like engineering, nursing, or pharmacy, virtually require a degree in a specific major in order to enter them, for most fields it is the candidate's skills and abilities that will determine whether he or she gets the job and is successful at it. This should be good news for college students. The major then takes on less importance. Knowing that they can acquire skills and experience that employers seek through a variety of ways, there is less pressure for students to choose the "right" major.

What are the skills that employers most frequently seek in new graduates? Obviously, these will differ depending on the particular field and job, but employers most often request the following skills:

- Computer skills (e.g., programming, familiarity with word processing and spreadsheet software)

- Quantitative skills (e.g., accounting, statistics, economics)

- Communication skills (written and oral)

- Required/Elective Courses
- Student Organizations/Activities

How to Gain Marketable Skills

- Volunteer Work   • Internships
- Jobs (part-time, summer, work-study, and self-employment)

- Marketing skills (selling, persuading)

- Scientific skills (laboratory, research)

- Foreign language skills

- Leadership skills

Since few individuals can excel in all of these areas, encourage your son or daughter to choose at least two or three of them to develop as strengths. These skills can be acquired through course work, volunteer or paid work, extracurricular activities, and other experiences such as studying or living abroad.

The Concept of Enhancers

The job market, like other economic markets, is based on supply and demand. The greater the supply of workers in a particular field in relation to the demand for those workers, the greater the difficulty in finding work in that field. Conversely, the greater the demand for workers in a field in relation to the supply of them, the easier it is to find work in that field. Let's look at two fields: broadcasting and mathematics teaching. Broadcasting is a very difficult field to enter because of the large supply of individuals wanting to enter it relative to the number of job openings. On the other hand, high school math teachers are in short supply; therefore, someone graduating with a degree in secondary mathematics education should not have much difficulty finding employment.

An individual may bring some "extras" in addition to the degree, which we call enhancers, to his or her candidacy. A student graduating from college with a basic liberal arts degree and little more is not likely to easily find a job in broadcasting. The student needs as many enhancers as he or she can possibly obtain.

What might these enhancers be? For the field of broadcasting, a list of desirable enhancers might look like this:

- Course work or major in radio or television or broadcasting

- Good grades

- Part-time job at the campus radio station

- Summer internships at a radio or television station

- Involvement in the campus student broadcasting association

It is important that as your son or daughter begins to focus on a career direction, he or she consider the supply–demand ratio for workers. The greater the supply of workers relative to the demand for them, the greater the need for enhancers. Fields for which enhancers are especially important are the arts, entertainment, communications, social services, museum work and historical preservation, and some areas of teaching (such as English, social studies, and physical education).

Enhancers

Extracurricular Activities

Contacts

Job-Relevant Skills

Grades

Job-Seeking Skills

Relevant Course Work

Work Experience/ Internships

5. Learning Job-Seeking Skills

Although many students think they can wait until their senior year to begin learning how to write a résumé, interview, and search for a job, these skills are important to underclassmen who will be applying for internships and part-time jobs.

We recommend that sophomores and juniors attend workshops in the career office on career planning and job search techniques.

Developing a Career Plan

Encourage your child to develop a career plan as a sophomore and to review it each year, making adjustments as necessary. The plan includes a list of projected activities, experiences, and skills to develop for the next two years along with an action plan indicating how the student will acquire them.

Todd was a student who enjoyed his English courses but wasn't sure about a career direction. He was considering several options such as writing, teaching, and public relations. He decided to major in English, since he thought he could do best in a subject he liked, but wanted to plan for a broad number of career possibilities upon graduation. The career plan he developed with the help of a career planning counselor in his college career office looked like this:

CAREER PLAN FOR TODD

Sophomore Year

- Declare English as a major

- Write for the school newspaper

- Volunteer for the campus Big Buddy program

- Take elective courses in public speaking, business communications, and public relations

- Join the student chapter of the Public Relations Society of America

- Research and make contacts in public relations, advertising, writing, and publishing

- Seek help from the career office on résumé-writing and interviewing

- Get a summer job (or unpaid internship) in a public relations or advertising firm

continued

Junior Year

- Take elective courses in computer skills (to learn word processing, desktop publishing, and graphics software)

- Continue to write for the campus newspaper; seek assistant editor position

- Work as a tutor for students having difficulty in English courses

- Take additional elective courses in public relations, advertising, and accounting (to acquire a valuable marketable skill)

- Do a course project related to a real-world public relations problem (possibly a marketing campaign for a university department, such as student health or the campus food service)

- Run for office in the campus public relations club

- Get summer internship in public relations firm

- Regularly read professional trade journals related to public relations and advertising (such as *O'Dwyer's PR Service Report* or *Advertising Age*)

By the time Todd was a senior, he had decided upon a career in public relations. Through the development and implementation of his career plan, he was in a strong position to fulfill his goal of finding an entry-level position in his chosen field. Had he decided to pursue some of his other interests, like publishing or teaching, he also would have strong credentials. (For a teaching career, though, he most likely would have to obtain certification or an additional degree, although there are some avenues to teach without either of these.)

A career plan will help your child better organize his or her time and be aware of what must be done over the sophomore and junior years to explore and prepare for career options. Like most of us, students are more likely to follow through on good intentions if they have a written plan of action with specific tasks and timetables. At the end of this chapter is a worksheet for a career plan, which you and your son or daughter can work on together. We suggest that your child discuss the plan with a college career counselor.

Recently a university created a program guaranteeing that students would have a job or admission to graduate school within six months after graduation or be paid $417 a month for up to one year. To be eligible for the plan, freshmen must sign a contract agreeing to attain a 2.75 GPA by graduation, participate in campus activities, complete an internship, and meet at regular intervals with a career counselor. Tom, a student who signed the contract, said, "If I want to get a good job, I've got to do this stuff anyway."

Tom is right. Colleges don't need to offer guarantees, and students don't need to sign contracts. A student who wants to find a good job has to do "this stuff"; and one who does is very likely to find a good job within six months of graduation, guarantee or no guarantee.

CAREER PLAN WORKSHEET

Sophomore Year

* Elective courses to develop marketable skills:

  _____

  _____

  _____

  _____

  _____

  _____

* Extracurricular activities to investigate/participate in:

  _____

  _____

  _____

  _____

* Career areas to explore:

  _____

  _____

  _____

* Information interviews to conduct:

  _____

  _____

  _____

* Seek help from counseling center or career office with _____

  _____

continued

- Part-time job:

  _____

- Apply for summer job or internship with _____

  _____

  _____

  _____

  _____

- Other:

  _____

  _____

  _____

Junior Year

- Major:

  _____

- Elective courses to enhance major/develop marketable skills:

  _____

  _____

  _____

- Extracurricular/volunteer activities and leadership roles:

  _____

  _____

  _____

  _____

- Information interviews:

  _____

  _____

  _____

  _____

continued

- Part-time work:

  _____

- Seek co-op or internship with _____

  _____

  _____

- Seek assistance from career office with _____

  _____

  _____

  _____

- Other (may include graduate/professional school investigation; admissions test preparation):

  _____

  _____

  _____

Summary

Timetable for Career Planning

Freshman Year

- Acclimate to college life
- Concentrate on making good grades
- Become involved in extracurricular activities

Sophomore and Junior Years

- Assess interests through testing
- Research careers of possible interest through reading and talking with those in the field

- Attend career days and other career-related programs sponsored by the campus career office

- Intensify involvement in extracurricular activities and assume leadership positions

- Gain career-related experience through volunteer work or extracurricular activities

- Obtain summer or part-time career-related work experience through paid or unpaid jobs and internships

- Develop marketable skills

- Build enhancers

- Develop a career plan

- Read professional trade journals in fields of interest

- Seek assistance from the career office with career planning, interviewing, and résumé writing

- Prepare for graduate/professional school

Marketable Skills

Develop strength in at least two or three of the following areas:

- Computer skills

- Quantitative skills

- Communication skills

- Marketing skills

- Scientific skills

- Foreign language skills

- Leadership skills

Gain marketable skills through:

- Required and elective courses

- Student organizations/activities

- Volunteer work

- Internships
- Jobs (part-time, summer, work-study, self-employment)

Enhancers

- Grades
- Extracurricular activities
- Contacts
- Marketable skills
- Job-seeking skills
- Relevant course work/course projects
- Work experience/internships

Conversation Starters for Parents and Students

1. Which campus activities do you think would interest you? Have you looked into joining them?

2. Which services does your career office offer to help students select a major or make career decisions?

3. Which summer jobs or internships do you think might be available to someone with your interests or major? Have you checked with the career office about how to obtain them?

4. Let's think about people we know in the fields which interest you (such as neighbors or relatives) so you can set up informational interviews with them.

5. Are you planning to attend career programs offered on campus? (If not, why not?)

6. Have you sought help from the career office in developing a career plan?

CHAPTER 2

STARTING OUT: FIRST JOBS FOR NEW GRADS (INCLUDING "HOT" CAREERS)

If you would be happy for a day, go fishing
If you would be happy for a month, get married
If you would be happy for a year, inherit a fortune
If you would be happy for life, love your work
—Chinese proverb

The top two reasons college freshmen give for attending college are "to get a better job" and "to make more money." Ironically, many students do not make the most of their college years to target a career and prepare for employment. They take the "Scarlett O'Hara" approach to career choices and say to themselves, "I'll think about it tomorrow." Some are easily discouraged by reports of a poor job market and wrongly assume that their efforts would be a waste of time. Other students believe a common myth, "You can't get a good job with just a bachelor's degree any more." They decide to focus their energies on graduate school applications and overlook many attractive job opportunities that do not require further education.

Even when students do explore career options, they often take a one-dimensional approach. They ask, "What are the highest paying jobs?" "What are the jobs that have the fastest growth?" As a result, some make decisions without regard to their natural abilities or sincere interests. One freshman had always demonstrated unusual artistic and writing ability. His parents were stunned to hear him announce that he decided to major in environmental science. His math and science grades, slightly above average at the high school level, did not seem to indicate great potential. But he had heard projections that environmental science would be a "hot" career field. His grades plummeted the next year in his new major.

A student's evaluation of career options may also be affected by peer pressure. Some students allow others (e.g., classmates, parents, or faculty) to unduly influence the process. Graduates often express regret at allowing themselves to be talked into (or out of) a career field. A student should ultimately make career decisions based on sound self-analysis as well as on field of interest.

Students sometimes avoid making a career choice because they are afraid of making the wrong decision, as if a career focus can never be changed. But members of Generation X are expected to change careers (not just jobs) an average of three or four times. So a first job does not signify a lifetime commitment but rather a starting point.

How can you help your child explore different career options? First, consider these questions:

- "What are my child's natural abilities—in what does he or she excel?"

- "Which types of activities motivate my child to do his or her best? When do I see sparks of passion and excitement?"

You want your child to be happy and successful in work. Ideally, your child will choose a career that is consistent with his or her strengths and abilities. However, students may have trouble being objective about their potential for different careers. As one said, "I want to be realistic, but I don't want to sell myself short either."

Reflect on your child's past successes. These achievements will give you some ideas about occupations to suggest. Did your daughter win a prize in a science fair? Perhaps she should consider becoming an engineer, chemist, or physicist. Did your son sell the most candy or raffle tickets for a school or youth group fund-raiser? He may want to consider using his persuasive skills as a lawyer, stockbroker, or advertising account executive.

Grades are also a good indicator of ability. If your child struggles with introductory biology and chemistry classes, then pre-med aspirations may not be realistic. Two-thirds of medical school applicants are turned down for admission, so even top students should have a backup plan if they aspire to become a physician. Some possible alternative career choices for pre-med students include health care consulting, pharmaceutical or medical equipment sales, technical or medical writing, laboratory research, and allied health fields such as nursing or physical therapy.

Students face heavy competition in the job market. However, some recruiters say that now is a good time for new graduates to begin their careers: employers are open to fresh new ideas as their organizations are being restructured. So talented new employees may make a greater impact than they did in previous years. On the other hand, employers' performance expectations are often higher than in the past. A poor job fit may be more likely to result in job loss or lack of advancement. It is important for your child to focus on his or her strengths and natural aptitudes when considering career options. Even though career changes are common, they are easier to make from related fields. For example, your son or daughter may want to make a future change from chemist to environmental consultant or from reporter to public relations representative.

Your child's values, interests, and personality traits are also important career choice factors. The type of motivation and traits required for success differ by field. Scientists must have a keen sense of curiosity and perseverance. They are driven by the prospect of discovering new knowledge. Sales professionals are self-motivated and competitive and value being able to measure their performance by objective results. (Recruiters often look for students who are active in competitive sports for management training programs in sales.) Social workers and educators find fulfillment in service to others. (Did your child enjoy tutoring other students or working as a camp counselor? Perhaps education or counseling would be the right field.)

For students interested in health careers, personality traits and aptitudes may point your child in the right direction within the field. A student with good science ability, manual dexterity, and mechanical aptitude may want to research opportunities in dentistry or prosthetics. Another, who excels in math and computer science and is not interested in patient contact, may want to pursue biostatistics.

Outstanding performers bring something extra to their jobs, perhaps through extraordinary effort, resourcefulness, or creativity. Parents can help their children identify what motivates them to go the extra mile, so that they are more likely to choose work at which they have a greater chance to succeed. Which of your child's accomplishments is he or she proudest of? How does he or she spend free time?

After targeting some career fields for exploration, your child may be tempted to make a choice that is based on limited information. One career field may offer high salaries for new graduates but be so competitive that successful candidates must have nearly a straight-A average. The job may also require frequent travel or relocation, long hours, and stressful working conditions. Another field that sounds glamorous or adventurous may offer low compensation. A new graduate can expect to make sacrifices and trade-offs when selecting a first job after college.

The Jobs Rated Almanac, by Les Krantz, is a helpful source that compares career fields by criteria such as income, job outlook, job security, and stress. Among the top 25 jobs are actuary, software engineer, computer systems analyst, accountant, paralegal, mathematician, computer programmer, parole officer, medical technologist, statistician, audiologist, hospital administrator, urban/regional planner, biologist, and industrial engineer.

Good Jobs for Undergraduates

Many students believe that there are no good jobs for students with an under-graduate degree. However, there are many options for new bachelor's-level graduates. Tables 2.1–2.9 at the end of this chapter provide an overview of typical job titles, starting compensation, predicted job growth from 1992 to 2005, and majors considered for entry-level jobs. The areas featured include accounting, banking, and finance; marketing and related fields; other business fields; science, math, and computer science; engineering and construction; health and related fields; government, education, and social services; communi-cations; and research (non-scientific). With proper preparation college gradu-ates in any major have many diverse job opportunities.

Although any major may qualify for numerous entry-level jobs, a student should target a few career fields and obtain related experience, college courses (such as electives or a minor), and skills to become competitive.

A bachelor's graduate with a more specialized background can become an accountant, engineer, computer programmer, nurse, physical therapist, or

ENTRY-LEVEL JOBS FOR ANY MAJOR

Banking management trainee	Purchasing agent	Production assistant
Customer service representative	Leasing agent	Special agent/ Inspector
Retail management trainee	Legal assistant	Probation officer
Sales representative	Claims adjuster	Administrative specialist
Assistant copywriter	Reporter	Credit manager trainee
Employee relations trainee	Underwriter	Assistant trader
Stockbroker trainee	Staff consultant	Membership representative
Legislative assistant	Financial analyst	Insurance agent
Hotel management trainee	Survey specialist	Restaurant management trainee

Customer Support Representative

Candidate wanted who will become an integral part of our dynamic team, performing various administrative support functions for our customer fulfillment office. Order entry, and accounts receivable. Must have: Liberal Arts or Business degree with demonstrated proficiency in problem solving. Excellent verbal and communication skills.

Admissions and Financial Aid Counselor

Major responsibilities of this entry-level position are student recruitment and financial aid counseling for a small college. The successful candidate must have a bachelor's degree and excellent communication skills. Opportunity to travel frequently.

Reporter/Associate Editor

San Francisco-based book publisher seeks bright, organized self-starter to handle day-to-day reporting duties for a weekly book industry newsletter. Must have demonstrable writing talent, journalism skills (including interviewing and reporting), and computer skills. BA in journalism or related field preferred.

Counselor

Responsible for working with behaviorally and emotionally troubled adolescents in an outdoor setting. This position is a 24-hour live-in position. Must have a BA/BS in Human Service field.

teacher, among other occupations. Some graduates choose to work for a year or two with nonprofit organizations like the Peace Corps, VISTA, or Teach for America. Others take appealing short-term jobs, such as teaching English in Japan or working for Club Med, Outward Bound, a cruise ship, or a dude ranch. (See Chapter 7.)

A Cautionary Note about Hot Careers

The job market is changing rapidly and is difficult to predict. A freshman may target a career field with high pay and plentiful opportunity but face very different prospects four years later. Engineering is an example of a field with a history of boom and bust cycles. Students may enroll in an area like aeronautical engineering to meet a short supply, only to face heavy competition upon graduation.

The nursing field is another example of a changing labor market. A shortage of nurses propelled their salaries upward in the early 1990s, and many hospitals offered a "bounty" to employees whose referrals resulted in hires. Nursing students mulled multiple job offers and were the envy of their classmates in less-specialized majors. But when the mid-1990s saw national health care reform proposals, hospitals responded to the uncertainty with cost-cutting measures. Their strategies included hospital mergers, layoffs of nurses, and substitution of lower-paid LPNs for registered nurses.

An ancient Chinese curse says, "May you live in interesting times." The pace of change will make these unpredictable years! Your child should choose a career direction that utilizes his or her strengths and matches his or her values and interests. Even if the job market undergoes unexpected changes, your child will have established a solid foundation for future career moves.

Hot Careers

Which fields appear most promising for those entering the job market? Futurists Alvin and Heidi Toffler describe three "waves" of change in history: the agrarian revolution, industrial revolution, and the information age. They write in the *Wall Street Journal* that "the Third Wave includes computer and electronics, biotechnology, and advanced manufacturing. It includes the increasingly data-drenched services, such as finance, software, entertainment, the media, advanced communications, medical services, consulting, training, and education—in short, all the industries based on mind-work rather than muscle-work.

Some occupations of the future undoubtedly do not exist yet. Others are still so new or unusual that there is not a big demand for applicants (for example, space-food scientists). Which jobs can current students target, and what are their prospects?

Tables 2.1–2.9 at the end of this chapter provide examples of common entry-level jobs obtained by recent college graduates. This chapter highlights ten occupations for their higher-than-average compensation, job market demand, or opportunities for growth. Most of these occupations are also regarded by college students as prestigious or especially attractive. They include the following:

- Research associate (junior consultant)
- Financial analyst (investment banking assistant)
- Physical therapist
- Pharmacist
- Engineer

- Computer programmer/Systems analyst

- Environmental scientist

Other positions requiring advanced degrees:

- Lawyer

- Physician

- Brand manager

Other hot occupations are accountant, financial manager, dentist, occupational therapist, health services administrator, applied mathematician (statistician, operations research analyst), chemist, biological scientist, financial services sales representative, and advertising account executive. International business is another growth area, one that is very popular with students. Some attractive career fields are described in more detail in the following section.

Consulting and Investment Banking

Can you imagine your child working 80-hour weeks? Does he or she earn top grades, and have outstanding analytical and quantitative skills?

Consulting and investment banking are high in mystique and glamour on college campuses. These industries attract many of the best students. Many parents are surprised to learn that the fields of consulting and investment banking are open to new bachelor's degree graduates.

Consulting firms seek students who have excelled academically. Some of them prefer course work such as computer science, engineering, other sciences, and business. New hires usually begin as staff consultants or business analysts. Consulting involves frequent travel and heavy overtime. An MBA is typically needed for advancement in management consulting (as opposed to systems

Associate Consultant	**Financial Analyst**
Conduct market research, qualitative and quantitative analysis, and assist in development and presentation of reports to clients. Requires a B.A. with course work related to economics, business, and statistics and record of academic achievement. Knowledge of Excel, Paradox, Powerpoint, and Word.	Fortune 500 financial services firm seeks bright, motivated, detailed-oriented applicants to join our team of financial analysts. Must have minimum 3.75/4.0 GPA and proven ability in mathematical work. Long hours, competitive salary, advancement opportunity.

consulting). Consulting firms frequently specialize in fields such as information systems, benefits and compensation, health care, and environmental work and may also recruit for advanced degrees related to these areas.

Investment banks value diversity in applicants' backgrounds but demand high GPAs (3.5 and above) and math aptitude as evidenced by SAT scores and college transcripts. New graduates typically begin as financial analysts. Training programs provide the specific skills new hires need for number-crunching and analytic work. An 80-hour work week is common in investment banking.

The duration of most financial analyst programs is two years, with a possible one-year extension for outstanding employees. The short-term commitment makes analyst jobs attractive to students who want to go to law school or obtain an MBA a few years after graduation. Financial analysts may earn over $100,000 in their two years of work from salaries and year-end bonuses. An MBA is almost always necessary to advance to associate and higher-level positions (also see Chapters 6 and 7.) Emerging or global markets is an investment banking area that may be especially attractive in the future, particularly for students with foreign language skills and an interest in international business.

Competition is keen for both consulting and investment banking jobs, and the work is very demanding. Both fields provide intellectual challenge, task variety, and lucrative compensation.

Law

Does your child have good analytic and persuasive skills? Feel comfortable in a confrontational setting? Enjoy research, writing, and public speaking or debate?

Law is a popular career interest for students, but law school admission is very competitive, and the job market for lawyers is tight. The Department of Labor expects rapid growth in openings for lawyers, but large law school enrollments will result in a continuing difficult job market for those who attend less prestigious institutions. Law schools award a J.D. degree after a three-year course of study.

Worth a Closer Look

Law	Paralegal
• Environmental lawyer • Intellectual property • Patent/Copyright lawyer • Labor and employment lawyer • Paralegal/Legal Assistant	Mid-sized Akron-area environmental law firm seeks college graduates with strong research and communication skills. Computer skills a must (IBM + Mac); law courses a plus.

Some specialties that appear to be growing are environmental law, intellectual property, copyright or patent law, and labor and employment law.

Paralegal and legal positions are also expected to continue to be in demand. Some law firms and government agencies hire graduates with any major and provide on-the-job training for these positions. Other employers prefer applicants who have completed paralegal training, which may be obtained through certificate programs in a few months or through degree programs lasting two to four years.

Health Professions

Does your child have an aptitude for science and an interest in helping people? Health professions are expected to be attractive careers in the 1990s and beyond. An aging population, increased interest in health and fitness, new technology, and the movement to managed care networks, such as HMOs, are trends that are increasing demand for health professionals. Physicians, physical therapists, and pharmacists are expected to be in demand because of this growth.

Medical school usually requires four years. An additional one to seven years of further medical education may be necessary in certain specialties. Physicians in primary care, medical research, reproductive endocrinology, and geriatrics appear to have especially good prospects.

Physical therapists receive training through either bachelor's or master's degree programs. An accredited bachelor's in pharmacy is a five-year degree, and hospitals are starting to prefer a Pharm.D., which takes another one to two years of study. Demand is also high for a number of professions that generally require post-graduate education: nurse practitioners, nurse-anesthetists, rehabilitation counselors, speech-language pathologists, audiologists, and health care administrators. Additional growth occupations not requiring postbaccalaurate study include physician assistants, occupational therapists, dieticians, nuclear medicine technologists, dental hygienists, respiratory therapists, and recreation therapists.

Clinical research and drug trials have created many opportunities for nurses, pharmacists, clinical laboratory technologists, biostatisticians, and programmers. Emerging health-related occupations include pharmacoeconomists and bioethicists, both requiring a graduate degree. Pharmacoeconomists analyze the cost-effectiveness of drugs and medical treatment. Bioethicists help health care professionals, lawyers, and families make decisions arising from new technology.

Engineering, Science, and Mathematics

Does your child excel in science and math? Have spatial ability and mechanical aptitude? Display characteristics such as perseverance, creativity, and attention to detail?

One in six new jobs from 1992 to 2005 will be filled by technical workers.

Engineering and Science

- Software programmer
- Network integration specialist
- Database manager
- On-line/Multimedia developer
- Electrical engineer
- Civil engineer
- Environment manager/ Industrial hygienist
- Operations research analyst
- Management information systems (MIS) specialist

Environmental Scientist

Washington-based firm specializing in energy and environmental issues seeks creative and resourceful environmental scientists with excellent problem-solving skills and a demonstrated ability to work under pressure and meet deadlines.

Requirements include a BA/BS in environmental or other science, public policy, or related field. Must be willing to travel. Fast-paced work environment, competitive salary, opportunity for advancement, and on-the-job training available.

Multimedia Developer

Participate in the design, development and roll-out of exciting new instructional applications on a client/server platform utilizing the latest in multimedia technology.

High level of creativity is a necessity. Graphic arts/ illustration experience, strong PC knowledge, and network skills. College degree preferred. Will consider all majors with related skills or experience.

Statistician

Responsible for performing quantitative analyses of clinical quality data from monitors using SAS, SPSSX for hospital center.

Requirements include a BS in Statistics or Business, or related field. A graduate degree preferred. Spreadsheets, word processors, relational database management/manipulation tools, statistical software, mainframe computer database tools, and graphics software. Clinical background (i.e., nursing, respiratory therapy, physical therapy) a plus.

Technological advances, global consumer demand for electronic products, and new regulatory requirements are causing an increased need for graduates with technical skills. There are plentiful opportunities for engineers in telecommunications, electric technology or electronics, computers, and environmental fields.

Computer scientists such as programmers, management information systems (MIS) specialists, and systems analysts are among occupations with the fastest growing rates as organizations use information systems to increase productivity and competitiveness. For example, medical informatics combines medicine and computer science for diagnostic purposes. Computer-based nursing is used for telephone triage in HMOs—to determine which patients need an appointment and which need an ambulance.

Environmental scientists have backgrounds in engineering, chemistry, or environmental science. They are employed by the government as environmental health inspectors and by industry as industrial hygienists and environmental managers to help organizations comply with government regulations regarding hazardous waste, pollutants, recycling, and other responsibilities.

Applied mathematicians such as statisticians and operations research analysts may expect strong job market demand as organizations use quantitative methods to improve productivity and make business decisions.

Opportunities are also predicted to be good for technical writers, who have both scientific and writing skills.

Marketing, Sales, and Distribution

Does your child have excellent persuasive skills? Is he or she a self-starter, competitive and results-oriented, with a high energy level? Sales or marketing may be a good career choice.

Global competition for consumer products is increasing the need for product or brand management employees. These marketing professionals oversee all aspects of promoting and distributing a particular brand, such as Ivory soap or Oreo cookies. Most brand managers have sales experience and an MBA. Some bachelor's degree recipients begin as a brand assistant, but most start as a sales representative.

Card Products Merchant Sales Representative	**Computer Sales Representative**
Make direct calls on merchants and cross-sell bank products in assigned territory. Must have college degree, computer competency, and willingness to travel.	Large audiovisual distributor seeks computer sales reps to handle various regions nationwide. BA/BS and basic computer literacy required.

Credit card marketing appears to be a promising field. On-line services marketing for companies such as Prodigy and CompuServe is becoming important as more households log on to the Internet.

Financial services sales is another growing field, due to baby boomers' reaching midlife and needing advice on savings and investments. An estimated $10 trillion in wealth is expected to be transferred from one generation to the next in a 50-year period (1990–2040).

Purchasing, distribution, and supply management are becoming important career fields because of their potential to strengthen companies' competitiveness. Procurement and purchasing managers are forging partnerships with suppliers to increase efficiency and cost savings.

International Business

Does your child have an aptitude for foreign languages and business? Plans to study or travel abroad? An ability to adapt to new circumstances?

Many students are interested in international business. Although the passage of NAFTA, the development of Third World and former Communist countries, and the unification of the European Community have increased American business interest in these markets, it is rare for an employer to hire a new graduate for an overseas business assignment. Work experience, language skills, and travel abroad may eventually lead to work in a foreign country. Some companies also prefer an MBA as an additional qualification.

The Big Emerging Markets (BEMs) identified by the Department of Commerce include ten countries:

- China
- Indonesia
- Mexico
- Brazil
- Poland

- India
- South Korea
- Argentina
- South Africa
- Turkey

By the year 2000 these countries are expected to form a larger U.S. export market than the European Union. Your child may want to target language and other studies accordingly if he or she is interested in international business.

Social Services and Education

Home health social workers, such as nurses with a master's degree in social work, will face plentiful job opportunities as managed health care providers serve an aging population in their homes. Psychologists, employee assistance

Placement Specialist	Overnight Counselors
B.S. in rehabilitation, social work, education or business required. Place persons with disabilities to work in restaurants throughout a multi-state area. Some travel required. Salary: $20,000 and up.	Awake overnight positions available in group homes serving adults with mental retardation. Both full-time (4-day week) and part-time (3-day week) positions available. BA and relevant experience preferred.

program counselors, and special education teachers may expect strong job market demand.

Commonly Overlooked Opportunities

Many students work as waiters or waitresses, hotel clerks, retail clerks, or bank tellers to finance their education. When management trainee openings occur in the hospitality, retail, or banking industries, they remember a low-level job with distaste and do not consider these career options. Yet some organizations in the hospitality and retail industries are among the fastest growing. The result is many missed opportunities by graduates.

Management trainees in retailing earn starting salaries averaging $20,000–$26,000 annually, with assistant managers earning $25,000–$33,000 plus bonuses. Retailing is an entrepreneurial environment, with rapid advancement possible in expanding companies. Store managers typically run a one- to two-million-dollar business and may earn $50,000 or more a year within three to five years of hire as a trainee.

Is your child a bookworm, computer hobbyist, or sports enthusiast? He or she could combine one of these interests with a career in a bookstore or an electronics- or sports-related retailer. Discount stores (such as Wal-Mart and Target) and "category killers" (including Toys 'R' Us and Baby Superstore) recruit on many college campuses. They usually prefer applicants with some retail experience, even if it is only part-time. Many restaurant, supermarket, and rental-car companies are also hiring management trainees. In addition to the store management career path, these companies offer opportunities in purchasing, computer science, human resources, and other staff positions.

Some hospitality and retail jobs involve lifestyle sacrifices. Work schedules may include evenings, weekends, and holidays, and promotions often require relocation. However, students may regret passing up a chance to interview for these management-track positions when they fail to find another job with career potential.

The insurance industry also receives less attention from job hunters because of misconceptions. Students often assume that insurance companies recruit only for sales positions, and they bypass many entry-level jobs in underwriting, claims, and other fields.

Potential for Income or Growth

Students with health-related majors who become pharmacists, nurses, dental hygienists, and clinical laboratory technologists typically earn among the highest starting salaries. However, these graduates may find that their earnings plateau fairly early. Additional education or entry to related career fields will often increase their opportunities. A Pharm.D. degree increases options for pharmacists. Nurses have opportunities to advance in hospital administration or in related areas as a nurse practitioner or physician assistant.

Although continuous learning is important for all workers, it is especially key for technical professionals. Engineers' skills become outdated quickly, but they can obtain an MBA or a master's in engineering to maintain their marketability and increase their income. Computer science professionals also need to continue their education to keep their skills from becoming obsolete.

Professionals who face modest entry-level salaries and limited growth prospects include teachers, paralegals, reporters, social service or nonprofit workers, and hospitality (hotel, restaurant, travel) workers. Some employees in these fields are exceptions, such as directors of large nonprofits, teachers with long service in top-paying school districts, paralegal specialists in large metropolitan law firms, and hospitality managers who advance quickly in fast-growth chains.

Some occupations with high earnings include physician, dentist, optometrist, attorney, investment banker, consultant, and stockbroker. It is important for your child to balance high potential income with other considerations such as the competition to enter a career, length of training, and other possible sacrifices. For example, medical school admissions is competitive, and physicians spend five to eleven years in medical school and residency programs. They graduate with educational debt of up to $100,000 and invest heavily if they establish a private practice. Self-employed physicians earn significantly more than those who work for others, but future opportunities are expected to occur chiefly in managed care settings, such as HMOs.

Professionals in some fields share in the profits of their firm through partnerships: this includes a select few in law, investment banking, consulting, and public accounting. (These are fields for which graduate degrees are typically necessary.) Designation as partner is not based on technical competence alone but is usually offered to those who also contribute by attracting new business to the firm. A large investment also is usually required from new partners.

Successful stockbrokers prosper through commissions, income that is based on a percentage of sales to clients. Turnover is high for new brokers, but this occupation is lucrative for outstanding performers who attract wealthy clients.

Job Security

Some jobs have been more recession-proof than others, including health care fields such as physical therapy, audiology, occupational therapy, and speech pathology. Computer science tends to be a field offering job security for programmers, systems analysts, and software engineers. Biological scientists often work on long-term research projects, which buffer them from ups and downs in the labor market. Law enforcement employees, such as parole and correctional officers, tend to be less likely to face unemployment than those in other occupations. Engineers, lawyers, insurance agents, claims adjusters, bill collectors, and accountants are also in occupations that offer better than average job security.

Even in many of these fields, employers often hire contract workers rather than permanent employees to allow maximum flexibility. As one employer put it, "Why should I hire an engineer to work for 30–40 years when his skills are obsolete so quickly? It is better to staff our projects through a contract firm with new graduates who know the latest technology." According to *Fortune* magazine, 3,000 computer programmers work at AT&T through contract organizations. Your child will work in a job market that rewards current and marketable skills. Job security, as most people think of it, is becoming an outmoded concept.

Starting Out: Entry-Level Jobs, Compensation, and Growth

Tables 2.1–2.9 contain average entry-level 1995 salaries; ranges (if available) include 10th to 90th percentiles. Information is derived from the National Association of Colleges and Employers' "Salary Survey" and the *Occupational Outlook Handbook*. Additional compensation for some fields may include bonuses and other incentives. Of course, these tables are not exhaustive; there are many other entry-level positions available to recent graduates.

Legend

Changing Employment Between 1992 and 2005

Much faster than average growth
Projected increase of **41% or more**

Faster than average growth
Projected increase of **27–40%**

Average growth
Projected increase of **14–26%**

Slower than average growth
Projected increase of **0–13% or decline**

Table 2.1
ACCOUNTING, BANKING, AND FINANCE

Field	Titles	Compensation	Job Growth	Typical Majors
Accounting	Staff accountant/Auditor General/Tax/Cost accountant	$24,000–33,000 $28,098 Avg	↑	Accounting
Banking Commercial	Management trainee Retail (branch) banking Credit (lending) Operations Loan processor Collections officer	$18,000–32,000 $25,156 Avg	↑	Any major Business Economics
Investment	Financial analyst Sales assistant	$23,000–36,000 $26,953 Avg		Any major
Finance/ Economics	Financial management trainee Budget analyst Financial analyst Economist	$20,000–35,000 $28,016 Avg	↑	Accounting Business/Public administration Economics Statistics
Insurance	Claims adjuster Underwriter	$20,000–32,000 $25,772 Avg	↑	Any major Business Insurance

Table 2.2
MARKETING AND RELATED FIELDS

Field	Titles	Compensation	Job Growth	Typical Majors
Advertising	Production assistant Assistant copy writer Media assistant	$15,080–28,500 $21,093 Avg	↑	Advertising Journalism, English Psychology Any major
Brand/Product Management	Brand assistant	$20,000–35,500 $26,962 Avg	↑	Business Any major
Retailing	Department manager trainee Assistant buyer	$22,000–30,500 $26,171 Avg	↑	Business Liberal arts Any major
Sales	Sales representative Telemarketer Stockbroker trainee Insurance agent	$18,500–35,000 $26,151 Avg	Varies by industry	Business Economics Sciences* Any major
Purchasing	Purchasing agent Contract specialist Buyer trainee	$23,000–31,200 $26,983 Avg	→	Business Economics Engineering Applied science Any major
Customer Service	Customer service representative Technical support representative	$15,000–27,500 $21,356 Avg	Not available	Sciences* Computer science Any major
Marketing Research	Coder/Editor Junior/Associate analyst	$20,000–35,000 $26,503 Avg	↑	Math/Statistics Business Economics

* For health or technical sales and service

Table 2.3

OTHER BUSINESS FIELDS

Field	Titles	Compensation	Job Growth	Typical Majors
Consulting	Staff consultant Business analyst	$27,996–38,000 $32,893 Avg	←	Computer science Applied math Business Any major
Hospitality	Hotel management trainee Restaurant/Food service management trainee	$22,000–28,000 $23,876 Avg	↑ ←	Hotel/Restaurant management Restaurant/Food service Any major
Human Resources	Staffing specialist Compensation analyst Employee relations trainee	$19,000–31,000 $24,312 Avg	↖	Business Industrial relations Any major
Real Estate	Leasing agent Assistant property manager Real estate analyst	$19,500–29,000* $28,933 Avg*	↑	Business Finance Real estate Any major
Production/ Operations	Production supervisor Operations trainee	$22,717–33,000 $27,179 Avg	→	Business Engineering Industrial Relations Any major

* Salary of business and real estate majors

Table 2.4
SCIENCE, MATH, AND COMPUTER SCIENCE

Field	Titles	Compensation	Job Growth	Typical Majors
Agriculture/ Natural Resources	Research assistant Soil scientist Cooperative extension agent	$16,800–30,000 $23,973 Avg	↑	Animal/Plant science Agricultural science Biology Other science, Engineering
Biological Sciences	Research assistant Biological technician	$15,080–30,000 $22,470 Avg	↗	Biology
Chemistry	Research technician Quality control chemist	$20,800–40,000 $30,115 Avg	↑	Chemistry
Mathematics and Applied Math	Mathematician Statistician Operations Research Analyst Research assistant/Analyst assistant Actuary	$30,110 Avg Not available $31,000–40,000 $35,354 Avg	→ ← ↑	Mathematics Statistics Computer science Operations Research Actuarial science Math, Statistics Economics Accounting/Finance
Computer Science	Programmer Software engineer Systems analyst Information systems specialist	$26,500–38,000 $32,352 Avg $27,500–38,000 $32,284 Avg $27,000–38,200 $32,198 Avg	↑ ← ←	Computer science Information science Engineering Math Business*

* For systems analysts

Table 2.5
ENGINEERING AND CONSTRUCTION

Field	Titles	Compensation	Job Growth	Typical Majors
Engineering	Civil engineer	$26,000–35,000 $30,707 Avg	↑	Civil engineering
	Electrical/Electronic engineer	$31,000–40,200 $36,230 Avg	↑	Electrical/Electronic engineering
	Chemical engineer	$34,200–44,000 $40,268 Avg	↑	Chemical engineering
	Computer engineer	$30,000–40,000 $35,659 Avg	←	Computer engineering
	Aerospace/Aeronautical engineer	$28,500–38,000 $32,831 Avg	→	Aerospace/Aeronautical engineering
	Mechanical engineer	$30,000–40,500 $35,956 Avg	↑	Mechanical engineering
Construction	Assistant project manager Cost estimator	$32,000 Avg	←	Construction science

Table 2.6

HEALTH AND RELATED FIELDS

Field	Titles	Compensation	Job Growth	Typical Majors
Nursing	Nurse	$24,000–45,000 $32,438 Avg	←	Nursing
Pharmacy	Pharmacist Assistant pharmacy manager	$40,000–56,000 $45,339 Avg	↑	Pharmacy
Medical Technology	Clinical laboratory technologist Medical technologist	$27,564 Avg	↑	Clinical laboratory science Medical technology Chemistry Biological sciences
Occupational Therapy	Occupational therapist	$33,948 Avg	←	Occupational therapy
Physical Therapy	Physical therapist	$35,667 Avg	←	Physical therapy

Table 2.7
GOVERNMENT, EDUCATION, AND SOCIAL SERVICES

Field	Titles	Compensation	Job Growth	Typical Majors
Government Executive and Legislative	Legislative assistant Research assistant	$23,535 Avg	→	Any major
Law Enforcement	Police officer Special agent	$18,000–34,000 $24,576 Avg	→	Administration of justice Any major
Regulation	Inspector Compliance officer	$18,707–23,171	↑	Science majors Any major
Military	Second lieutenant Ensign	$29,688*	→	Engineering Any major
Social Services	Parole/probation officer Claims examiner Compliance specialist EEO assistant	$18,707–23,171	↑	Psychology Sociology Business Any major
Education	Preschool teacher Elementary teacher Special education teacher	$16,640–27,500 $22,468 Avg	↑	Education Alternative certification in Chemistry, Biology, Foreign languages
Nonprofit/Private Social Services	Residential counselor Shelter manager Habilitation specialist Teaching parent Fund-raiser	$13,000–25,700	←	Psychology Sociology Any major

* Including allowances

Table 2.8
COMMUNICATIONS

Field	Titles	Compensation	Job Growth	Typical Majors
Reporting	Reporter	$18,092 Avg	↑	Journalism English Any major
Public Relations	Public relations specialist	$18,000–30,000 $21,875 Avg	↑	Public relations Journalism Any major
Writing and Editing	Technical writer Editorial assistant	$15,600–25,000 $20,199 Avg	↑	English Journalism Any major Sciences*
Production	Product assistant Camera operator Announcer Reporter	$15,080–28,000 $23,586 Avg	↑	Broadcast journalism Any major

* For technical writing

Table 2.9

OTHER RESEARCH (NONSCIENTIFIC)

Field	Titles	Compensation	Job Growth	Typical Majors
Legal Research	Paralegal Legal assistant	$18,200–24,400 $21,571 Avg	←	Any major Paralegal certificate/degree programs
Research, Nontechnical	Survey specialist	$18,500–33,400 $24,172 Avg	↑	Any major Math Statistics

Summary

Factors to Consider in Career Choice:

- Job duties
- Advancement opportunities
- Compensation and benefits
- Job market demand
- Aptitude and motivation
- Working conditions

Hot Career Fields:

- Can be difficult to predict and subject to rapid change
- Are likely to be found in professional business services, health professions, science or computer science, and marketing or sales

Ten Hot Careers

Consultant	Pharmacist
Investment banker	Engineer
Lawyer	Computer programmer/Systems analyst
Physician	Environmental scientist
Physical therapist	Brand manager

Entry-Level Jobs for Bachelor's Graduates

- Available to any major in a wide variety of fields
- Available to specific majors in more technical fields

Conversation Starters for Parents and Students

1. What do you consider your biggest accomplishment? Which of your activities do you enjoy the most? What achievement or activity has made you feel most proud of your efforts?

2. What is your favorite course? Is it also the course where you earned the best grades? If not, why not?

3. How would you describe the ideal job for you?

4. What are some of the advantages of career choices you have considered? What are some of the risks or disadvantages?

5. How would some of your career options affect other aspects of your life, such as family, hobbies, and volunteer work?

CHAPTER 3

CHOOSING A MAJOR: DRAMA VERSUS ACCOUNTING

Don't despair if your child is having difficulty choosing or staying with a major. More than half of college freshmen are undecided about their major, and it is estimated that over three-fourths of all college students change their major at least once while in college. Some students change their major so frequently they could quality for the "Major of the Month Club!"

Eventually, though, and at most schools by the end of the sophomore year, your son or daughter will have to select a major, even if only temporarily. And sooner or later, if he or she is to graduate, one major will have to be settled upon. How should it be done?

Like choosing a career, there is unfortunately no magic formula or test to give the answer. But there are some important considerations. The self-assessment and career research discussed in Chapter 1 will help narrow down possible career options. The career choice, if known early enough, may define the major. Architecture, engineering, education, and many of the health and allied health fields (such as medical technology, pharmacy, and physical therapy), are examples of fields in which the career and major are identical. Even these fields, though, can be entered later through other routes (such as programs of study as short as one year after a bachelor's degree), so it is not essential that a student major in them in order to ever work in them.

A known career choice may also suggest *several* possible majors, giving the student the option to choose the one that is most appealing. For example, the student interested in a sales career might major in business, psychology, or communications.

Students may initially select a major based on a hobby or interest and may consider making a career of this interest. They may find, though, that studying a subject is different from having an avocational interest in it. The student who enjoys tinkering with cars, stargazing, or working with animals may discover that the rigorous disciplines of mechanical engineering, astronomy, or zoology are not what he or she wants to study for four or more years.

What if your child is undecided upon a career or is thinking of careers in radically different disciplines: music versus math? Keeping in mind that he or she probably has about two years before having to declare a major, encourage your child to take several courses in areas of interest. An introductory course in anthropology or accounting may spark a desire to pursue these subjects further, or a few courses in music may help your child realize that majoring in math would be preferable.

A student who is still having trouble choosing between two majors of interest after having taken a few courses in both might want to base the decision on the employment demand for the majors, information that can be obtained from the career office. Although students with the proper preparation can find satisfactory work regardless of their major, students in some majors are likely to have less difficulty than others.

Cary, a sophomore, was interested in both philosophy and business. After research and discussion with his career and academic advisers, he decided to major in business, the more "marketable" degree, but to continue to take philosophy courses as his schedule would allow.

Another student, Emily, enjoyed her courses in biology and journalism. She chose journalism as her major and supplemented it with biology and other science course work in order to prepare for a career as a science writer.

Students should major in something they enjoy. Not only are they more likely to stick with it, but they will also make better grades, have greater interest, and not look at the academic side of college merely as something they must endure as a means to an end—a diploma. Of course, students may basically enjoy the major they have chosen yet still encounter a particular course, professor, or required elective that they intensely dislike. Sometimes they *do* have to endure it as a means to an end! For example, students majoring in the sciences, health disciplines, or computer science may be required to take organic chemistry, physics, or calculus. These courses can be quite difficult for many students and can scare students out of the major. Also, some students avoid math and science courses because faculty in these disciplines usually have a reputation for grading more stringently.

If the problem is only with one or two courses and the student can get through them, possibly with tutoring, he or she should not be scared off. On the other hand, a change of major should be considered if the major will require many courses in subjects that he or she finds extremely hard or uninteresting. (Sometimes the decision to change is essentially made for students because they are unable to pass the course needed to advance to the next level.)

Which Comes First—The Major or the Career Choice?

Is it better to choose a major based on one's career interest or to choose a career based on one's major? This is a chicken-or-egg question. Some students could not possibly base a decision about their major on their career interests because their interests are still very vague. These students typically choose a general liberal arts major, like psychology, biology, or political science. Those who have fairly well defined career interests are likely to select a major that relates at least minimally to those interests: the student interested in advertising may choose to major in English or journalism; the student interested in computer programming may major in mathematics or computer science; or the student interested in social services may major in psychology or sociology.

Students may incorrectly assume that a particular major is required or desirable for their career goal. For example, students interested in careers in investment banking sometimes think that they should major in business. Actually, investment banks recruiting bachelor's-level candidates usually prefer liberal arts majors with exceptionally high grades and test scores (on standardized exams such as SAT, GRE, LSAT, and GMAT).

Often students aspiring to law school believe that political science or history is the best major to choose. In reality, there are no *required* majors for admission, although law school admission officers *recommend* majors—or at least course work—in areas that demand rigorous logic and problem solving, like philosophy, chemistry, and accounting.

Students planning to apply to MBA programs often mistakenly think that an undergraduate major in business is best, but business schools usually prefer any major *except* business. Exceptions are the few MBA schools that have accelerated programs (one year rather than two) for students with undergraduate business majors.

Many medical schools no longer require a science or pre-med major, although they do require several specific science courses.

Students should check with the career office, employers, graduate or professional school admissions officers, people working in fields of interest, as well as other students and faculty in the prospective major before making a final decision about their major.

Selecting a Major that Isn't Career Related

Parents may worry if their child wishes to choose a major that doesn't readily point to a career or is in a field that seems impractical or impossibly competitive.

Their children pick up on these fears. "You would just *die* if I became a theater major, wouldn't you?" Stacey, a junior in high school, asked her mother. The truth is, her mother (one of the authors) didn't die: Stacy graduated from college as a theater major and is now successfully working in musical theater, with her mother being one of her proudest supporters.

Career counselors often see students who want to major in a liberal arts field like art or history, but whose parents want them to major in business or some other applied major. Some parents even threaten to withdraw financial support if their child doesn't major in something that the parents consider practical.

It is natural to worry about whether our children will be able to find a job once they graduate. (If there weren't a need to be concerned, this book wouldn't be necessary.) But the major itself is rarely the cause of a graduate's difficulty finding employment. It is true that a few majors, like special education, pharmacy, or chemistry, are very much in demand (as of this writing), so graduates of these majors generally find jobs easily; however, most students who plan well and have decent grades can find work regardless of their major.

There is a direct relationship between the college major and job upon graduation for only about 50% of college graduates. (The number is higher for certain fields, like accounting, engineering, and nursing.) Later in a graduate's career, the job is even less likely to be related to the graduate's major. So although the communications or philosophy major may not necessarily be employed in his or her field, the major is itself not a one-way ticket to unemployment or underemployment.

At many colleges, such as the University of North Carolina and the University of Florida, more employers who recruit on campus request to interview "any major" than any single major like computer science or business. This does not mean, though, that recruiters will interview any candidate: they are quite particular about whom they will see. Although the request may not specify a particular major, it often does specify a certain GPA, work experience (part-time work or internship), and course work such as six hours of accounting. The career plan and enhancers discussed in Chapter 1 can make a great difference in a senior's being able to obtain campus interviews and in the success of those interviews.

When an Early Choice of Major Is Optimal

During the first two years your son or daughter will probably be taking primarily liberal arts or general education courses unless he or she has decided upon a major that requires early prerequisites or courses that must be taken in sequence. A freshman or sophomore who has already decided to major in a field such as business, accounting, engineering, architecture, science, mathematics, computer science, or health sciences should enroll as early as possible in the courses required for the major: often these majors require many prerequisites. Your son or daughter's academic adviser will help him or her select the courses required.

Students who have not yet made a definite decision but are considering majoring in engineering, mathematics, science, or health sciences should take the more difficult math courses (e.g., calculus) and organic chemistry (for those with interests in science or health) as freshmen or sophomores; otherwise they may find their options to major in these subjects limited or may have to backtrack in order to obtain the necessary prerequisites.

Some students change their major so often that they have far more credits than they need to graduate by their senior year yet do not have the required courses in the major they have finally settled on. They may need to stay as much as one or two additional years in order to obtain the "right" credits.

Getting Accepted into the Desired Major

A few colleges or universities accept students directly into their desired major or "school" during the admissions process. Students attending these institutions, therefore, are assured as freshmen that they may enroll in the School of Business, School of Design, or School of Education, for example. Most colleges and universities, though, do not require students to declare a major before their sophomore year. This is an advantage because it allows students to explore various subject areas without feeling pressure to make an early decision; yet it can be a problem for students without high grades who want to major in a discipline that has limited enrollment. Many colleges have a limited number of spaces in majors such as architecture, engineering, business, accounting, and the health areas (like pharmacy, nursing, and physical therapy). Students must generally apply as sophomores for admission to these programs. Admission usually requires a minimum GPA of 2.7 or 3.0 as well as an application that may ask for an essay and information about work experience or extracurricular activities. Students considering majors with limited enrollment should seek information as early as possible, preferably as freshmen, in order to know what they will need to be competitive for admission.

What if your son or daughter is denied admission to the major he or she wants? Our first recommendation is to talk to the dean or administrator of the program; ask why admission was denied and discuss the possibility of reapplying. Sometimes a student can improve grades or acquire sufficient work experience (through volunteer or part-time work) in order to be admitted in a semester or so. It is important for the student to assess, with advice from the program administrator, how likely it is that he or she will be admitted within a reasonable period of time. Some students stay on and on at a college, continuing to hope that they will gain admission to the School of Design, for example, and never do. In the meantime they may have spent six or more years of time (and their *parents'* money) instead of being realistic and moving on with an alternative plan.

One alternative might be to select another major that is close to the desired one and will allow the student to enter his or her chosen career field. An example of this is to major in economics or industrial relations if admission to the business major is denied. Another option is to choose a less-competitive major in a similar career field, such as choosing occupational therapy rather than the highly competitive physical therapy. A third option is to take course work or to "minor" in the desired area. Students denied admission to an accounting program, for example, will find that six to nine hours of accounting coursework is sufficient for many employment opportunities in banking and finance. A last alternative is to transfer to an institution where admission to the desired program is less competitive. Counselors from the university counseling center and career office can help students explore their options.

The Importance of Grades

When selecting a major, students should consider how well they are likely to do in it and how important grades are for their intended career. A recent study by the Collegiate Employment Research Institute indicates that over 59 percent of employers require a minimum GPA of 3.0 for new graduates. If your child is struggling in a major and is barely able to maintain a 2.5 GPA, he or she might consider changing to a less difficult major.

It can be particularly difficult for students with low GPAs in majors like mathematics, chemistry, physics, accounting, and engineering to find employment in fields related to their major, especially when the job market is competitive. Certain career fields like consulting and investment banking are open to any major but require very high grades (typically over a 3.4). Students considering graduate or professional school, for which a high GPA is usually important, should select a major that will both meet the course requirements for the graduate program in which they are interested and will be one in which they can excel.

Your son or daughter may have a strong interest in a subject and wish to major in it in spite of the fact that he or she isn't making high grades. Not all fields or employers emphasize grades. Fields like sales, retail, hospitality, and the arts, as well as smaller employers, tend to value experience and demonstrated interest over grades. Nevertheless, it is important to check in advance to know the consequences of low grades. Your son or daughter can obtain this information by talking with potential employers, people working in fields of interest, and the career office.

How Useful Are Minors?

Most students take only about one-quarter to one-half of their course work in their major. They may be required to take many other courses in order to meet requirements of the general university or of the particular school that houses their major. For instance, often the School of Humanities or Liberal Arts requires two years of a foreign language, whereas the School of Engineering or Business may not. Some universities also require, or at least allow, a minor. Minors can enhance a student's credentials if they are selected wisely. For example, a student wanting a career in international affairs might major in political science and minor in a language like Spanish or Russian. Minors can also be an alternative route to a major that may not be offered: a student interested in management information systems attending a college that does not have this major can simulate it by majoring in computer science and minoring in business, or vice versa.

Students may be required or permitted to select a concentration, special option, or track within their major. Examples are a business administration major with a concentration in finance or a mathematical sciences major on the statistics track. Concentrations, tracks, and options allow students to develop strength and specialization in an area of interest.

The Interdisciplinary Major

Some colleges offer the option of an "interdisciplinary major," which can serve the same purpose as a major-minor combination. Usually the interdisciplinary major consists of course work from three subject areas combined in a planful way; this major must be approved by the student's academic adviser. Karen, a student at a large university without a major in hospitality, was interested in convention management. She received approval for an interdisciplinary major in business, psychology, and recreation administration. In addition to her major, she prepared a career plan that included volunteer work and internships at a hotel owned by her university and at the university's activities center, which sponsored many concerts and large events. Upon graduation she was hired as an assistant to a city convention manager.

What about Double Majors?

How useful are double majors? Students often assume that if one major is good, two are twice as good. Like minors, double (or even triple!) majors can be helpful if the student has a particular career goal in mind. A double major

Table 3.1
POSSIBLE MAJOR-MINOR COMBINATIONS

Career Choice	Major	Minor
Technical writing	English or Journalism	Chemistry, Biology, or Computer science
Computer systems consulting/Management information systems	Business	Computer science
Sports management	Business	Physical education or Recreation administration
Pharmaceutical sales	Business or Economics	Pharmacy or Biology
Health administration	Health area (e.g., Nursing, Health education)	Business or Economics
Arts management	Art or Art history	Business or Economics
Market research	Statistics	Business or Economics
Computer graphics	Computer science	Art
Government/Public administration	Political science	Business or Economics

(Major or minor can be reversed)

in health policy and business, for example, is ideal for the student interested in hospital administration. Similarly, a double major in advertising and economics is desirable for a student wanting to enter the noncreative side of advertising, such as being an account executive. However, a double major in psychology and sociology or in history and political science rarely enhances a student's qualifications in the eyes of employers. Of course a student may wish to double-major or take an optional minor for the intellectual stimulation or simply to study a second area in depth.

Often students have to work tremendously hard to meet all of the requirements for two majors. They may have many labs or special projects like art shows or music performances that can be very time consuming. Striving to meet the demands of two majors may cause a student to have lower grades, participate in fewer extracurricular activities, and feel a great deal of stress. It can delay a student's graduation by as much as a year. In a survey of 30 campus recruiters, only two thought that a double major improved a student's credentials. Students should carefully consider the costs versus the payoff of a double major.

B.A. versus B.S.

In some fields, like math or chemistry, students must choose between the bachelor of arts (B.A.) and the bachelor of science (B.S.) tracks. Usually the B.A. track has fewer required courses in the major and is considered more of a general liberal arts degree. It is the degree typically chosen by students planning to go directly to graduate or professional school or by those who want the flexibility of choosing more electives outside their major field. The B.S. degree is preferred by employers seeking bachelor's-level candidates in math and science, and by admissions officers of graduate programs in these fields.

Use of Electives

Even with the number of courses students must take for their major, their minor (if they choose one), and the university requirements, they still have many electives from which to choose to achieve the required hours for graduation. Judicious use of these electives can make students both better educated and more marketable. We recommend that *all* students take courses in these six subjects:

- Basic writing (particularly business writing)
- Public speaking
- Computer literacy (word processing, desktop publishing, and spreadsheet software)
- Foreign language (a minimum of two years)
- Business or economics (a minimum of one to two courses)
- Accounting (one to three courses)

Some of these courses (e.g., accounting) may not be offered at all colleges or universities, or they may be difficult to obtain because space is reserved for majors only. Students can investigate alternative routes, such as enrolling at another institution close by (some neighboring schools even have agreements that allow students to do so at no additional cost), taking the courses at a community college or at their own school in the summer (when access may be easier), or enrolling in a summer business institute (see Chapter 6).

Students should select other electives according to their career plan in order to obtain the knowledge and skills for their field of interest and to add to their qualifications as a prospective employee (as discussed in Chapter 1). Obviously, some electives should be chosen to explore other areas of interest.

Preparing for a Global Society

With virtually every large business (and many smaller ones as well) entering the global marketplace, employers are emphasizing foreign language skills and international and intercultural experiences as never before. Languages currently most in demand by employers are Spanish, Chinese, Russian, and Portuguese. Knowledge of one foreign language improves the ability to learn others; therefore, even if your child selected one language to study and later finds that a different one would have been better for his or her field, the time and effort learning the language will not have been wasted. Many graduate and professional schools also require, or at least value, foreign language skills.

Language skills alone, however, do not open many doors to jobs other than teaching. There are few opportunities to work strictly as a translator or interpreter, and native speakers or individuals who are proficiently bilingual (or multilingual) are usually sought to fill these. Knowledge of a language should be combined with other marketable skills.

International travel and study broaden students' horizons and help them develop fluency in a foreign language. International experience and language skills can be especially helpful for some careers, like art history, archaeology, foreign language teaching, the travel industry, customer service, the Peace Corps, the Foreign Service, and government intelligence (e.g., the FBI or the CIA), and can give students an edge over other applicants. Nevertheless, candidates must have additional marketable skills in order to be in a strong position for entry-level employment.

Many students are so eager to travel abroad that they do so without fully considering the consequences of missing a semester on campus or a summer internship. Students interested in a semester abroad should make sure that they will not miss necessary courses offered only in the semester in which they are overseas. Also, students should avoid being off campus in their senior year so that they will not miss campus interview opportunities. Summer travel is best done between the freshman and sophomore years, when students are less likely to be able to obtain significant work experience or internships. It is not advisable for students, especially juniors, to choose summer travel over an internship. Employers don't tend to look favorably on students who graduate without a job and spend months traveling before seeking employment.

Academic Honors

It is quite special for a student to be awarded academic honors. Academic scholarships, the Dean's List, university or department honors programs, and academic honorary societies and awards demonstrate that your child stands out among his or her peers in terms of academic achievement. These programs and awards challenge, stimulate, and motivate the superior student, and they are highly valued by many employers. Students who have the option to participate in honors programs and elect to do so should be aware, however, that the demands may be great in terms of time and effort.

Sometimes students who have earned honors don't realize that they should proudly claim them; in fact, they may dismiss opportunities to do so because they cost a minimal amount of money or effort. Jason, a sophomore at a costly private university, casually mentioned to his parents that he had received a letter of invitation for an honorary society of his major, speech, but chose not to join because it cost $25. His parents quickly told him that they would gladly pay the fee and hoped it wasn't too late to do so. "Do you really think we wouldn't pay an extra $25 to allow you to claim an honor which you've worked so hard for?" they asked him. Jason hadn't thought about the value of being a member of an academically elite group and also of being able to list the honor on his résumé later.

As desirable as academic achievement is, though, high grades and honors without work experience, leadership roles, and marketable skills will not prepare today's graduates to be competitive in the job market.

How Parents Can Help

It is important for you to listen to your son or daughter's thoughts about choosing a major. Some students want to talk with their parents frequently about their major or career, whereas others don't want to think about or discuss these issues. In either case try to be patient and supportive. Encourage open discussion about why your child is considering a particular major and what he or she hopes to accomplish by choosing it. Help your child think through issues such as course options and requirements, academic demands, reputation of the department, and relevance to career goals.

Students may have some anxiety about making these important decisions. Many seem to choose a major by waiting until the last possible moment and then throwing a dart at a list of majors offered. Assure your child that the decision is not irrevocable. What is key is that he or she not procrastinate about exploring the issues and gathering information to make an informed decision.

Keep in mind that students differ widely in their readiness to make decisions about their major and career and that most students will change their major at least once. Raise questions and concerns in a nonjudgmental way, showing your interests in helping your child make the best decision *for him or her* and one that will aid in achievement of *his or her* goals.

Summary

Factors to Consider When Selecting a Major

- Students should major in a subject they enjoy

- Students should major in something in which they can do well

- Parents should not worry if the major isn't career related (but encourage their student to develop and follow through on a career plan)

Minors/Interdisciplinary Majors

- Students can "construct their own major" through use of a major plus a minor or through an interdisciplinary major

Double Majors

- Students may double-major for specific career or personal goals

- Double majors aren't generally valued by employers unless they specifically relate to the employer's needs

Use of Electives

Students should choose electives:

- To explore possible majors

- To gain marketable skills

- To enhance their qualifications

- According to their career goals and plan

Importance of Grades

High grades are usually necessary for:

- Employment related to math, chemistry, physics, accounting, and engineering
- Careers such as consulting and investment banking
- Graduate/professional school admission

Most employers seek new graduates with a 3.0 or higher GPA

Role of Honors

- Students should strive to attain academic honors
- Students should join academic honorary organizations if they qualify
- Honors are impressive to most employers
- Honors and high grades without work experience, leadership roles, and marketable skills aren't sufficient to lead to employment

Helping Your Child

Parents should:

- Encourage open communication about majors and careers
- Not be judgmental about the student's choices
- Be patient and supportive, but raise important questions and issues

Conversation Starters for Parents and Students

1. Which college classes have you enjoyed the most? Why?
2. When do you have to declare a major?
3. Have you talked with your academic adviser and a counselor in the career office about choosing a career? What was their advice?

4. Which majors are you considering? Why these?

5. Do you think you are likely to do well academically in the major you are considering?

6. Which major or majors do you think would best prepare you for your career goals?

7. Which electives do you think would best complement your major?

CHAPTER 4

How Long Should It Take?

"So, have you started to think about your plans after graduation next year?" Tom O'Reilly looked hopefully at his son Robert, a college junior.

"I think I'm going to need more time. Hardly anybody graduates in four years these days. It doesn't look like I have enough credits to finish next year. Besides, I'm thinking of getting a double major. I might be able to do it in four and a half years, five at the most," Robert replied.

While some students push themselves to graduate early, others aren't in any hurry to finish their bachelors degree. How long *should* it take?

Not surprisingly, parents and their children often have different perspectives on the length of time needed to complete college. Parents generally assume that less is more. While they spend less money for tuition, living expenses, and books, their son or daughter earns more income by beginning full-time employment sooner. Less time in college seems even more advantageous if a student is contemplating graduate or professional school. Finally, let's not overlook the bragging potential of telling all of their friends that their child is graduating in "only three years."

Students, on the other hand, may not be in any hurry to leave college for the real world, with all its uncertainties. They may want to take a light load to keep their grades as high as possible, to squeeze in many extracurricular activities, or simply to allow for an active social life.

There is no one answer that is right for every student. Graduating early (in less than four years) is not necessarily good, nor is graduating late (in more than four years) necessarily bad. In making that decision, it is important to consider your son or daughter's particular situation and goals, as well as the advantages and disadvantages of graduating "off schedule."

Graduating Early

Susan, a college senior, looked down at the draft of her résumé with disbelief. It looked so skimpy, somehow.

Her college career counselor prompted her optimistically, "What about work experience—internships, summer jobs, or part-time employment? Have you done any volunteer work or been involved in any extracurricular activities?"

"No. No. No. I didn't have time because I'm finishing in three years."

"I see," remarked the counselor, confident that there was surely something that Susan had forgotten to list on her résumé and that he would help her find it. "What about academic honors, such as the Dean's List?"

"Yes, but only once," Susan conceded. Although she was a top student in high school, her college transcript was respectable but not exceptional.

Some students speed through college as if in a race against time, completing a bachelor's degree in as little as two and a half to three years. Why do they graduate so quickly and how do they do it?

Why Students Graduate Early

College Preparatory Classes

Some students who take college-level classes in high school do not expect to need the traditional four years to complete a bachelor's degree. If they don't feel sufficiently challenged by their course work, they may graduate early. These students have often been academically gifted from an early age. They—and their parents—assume that if it takes most college students four years to graduate, surely *they* can do it in less time.

Advanced Placement

Very bright students often begin college with a head start; they pass advanced placement (AP) tests or enter with credits obtained at a local college while enrolled in high school. Students may "place out" of nearly two semesters of college work. However, this route presents potential disadvantages, which students usually do not anticipate. Since they receive credit for introductory courses, they may choose to enroll in upper-level courses. Once in a course, they may find that by skipping the prerequisite course they missed an important concept that is key to their understanding the material. This can be especially problematic in courses required for a student's major; therefore, we do not recommend that a student place out of courses in the major, even if they are eligible to do so.

First-year students enrolled in upper-level courses are competing for grades with juniors and seniors while adjusting to college life as freshmen. The first year of college is usually difficult for students. High school valedictorians are now classmates. Good grades may not come as easily as they once did: parents are not close by to ensure good study habits; there are more distractions than in high school; competition is stiffer; and classes may be bigger and more impersonal.

Successfully passed AP tests count toward credit hours; however, grades on these tests are not factored into a student's GPA. Again, this may be a disadvantage that accompanies the head start on college. Instead of receiving A's in introductory courses, a student may earn Bs and Cs in higher-level courses. The former high school valedictorian may not even qualify for the Dean's List, despite high expectations.

Kevin entered college with so many AP credits that he was classified as a sophomore. But his first year away from home, he had difficulty adjusting socially and emotionally, which affected his grades. Although he was a stellar student in high school, his difficulty in adjusting, combined with the rigorous academic demands of upper-level courses, resulted in a mediocre GPA of 2.6 his first year. The following year Kevin studied in France, earning better grades; however, although the credits for his courses at the University of Lyons were accepted by his state university, his grades did not transfer. When Kevin returned to campus for his third and final year, his GPA remained at the 2.6 he earned his first year. This student who had seemed so promising as a freshman now appeared very average to employers and was unable to even obtain interviews with recruiters in his desired field—investment banking.

Heavy Course Loads

A student may accelerate college by taking more credit hours than average (possibly 18–21 hours per semester as opposed to 12–15). Grades may suffer, though, with less study time available for each class. In addition, a heavy course load may preclude or decrease involvement in extracurricular activities and part-time employment. Since many courses have prerequisites, early graduation may also limit a student's options for electives, since all courses are not offered each term.

Summer School

Students attending summer school for two or three summers may be able to graduate at least one or two terms early. These students may complete college without any work experience, putting themselves at a disadvantage, since employers place increasing importance on experience related to a student's career goals. Summer internships provide valuable experience for students who are available for work. As an alternative, students attending summer school several summers should obtain career-related experience during the school year through part-time jobs, volunteer work, or other sources.

Graduate School Plans

Students sometimes regard a bachelor's degree as merely a necessary prelude to graduate school. Why not speed things up, they reason. The more quickly they can complete their undergraduate studies, the sooner they can begin graduate work. For some students this reasoning is sound; they save time and a substantial amount of money. Others, however, experience burnout and decide to take time off before continuing their studies. They may find themselves drifting for a year or two, unable to obtain significant work because they have little more to present to employers than high grades.

Some universities offer qualified students the opportunity to combine an undergraduate with a graduate or professional school degree: for example, a business major may be able to combine his senior year with his first year of MBA work, resulting in a savings of one academic year and a significant amount of tuition money, and the opportunity to begin working one year earlier than most MBAs. Or, a pre-med student may be able to enroll in medical school after only three years of undergraduate education. These accelerated programs are only available at a few institutions, and only students with the strongest qualifications are admitted to them.

Financial Savings

The cost of a college education can run over $100,000 at private institutions and $30,000 at public ones (particularly for out-of-state students). Students may rush through their academic work for financial reasons. Several colleges have initiated special programs to allow students to graduate in three years or less and have predicted tuition savings of up to $25,000. Albertus Magnus College, for example, has begun a program with a three-term ("tri-session") academic year. Students may graduate in two and two-thirds years. Some colleges offering a three year bachelor's degree are Drury College, Middlebury College, Upper Iowa University, and Valparaiso University. The University of Arizona and the University of Wisconsin are two schools that allow qualified students to begin master's-level studies before completing the bachelor's degree.

Impact of Graduating Early

Prospective employers and graduate and professional schools have mixed reactions to early graduation. On the one hand, it is an accomplishment and shows commitment to a difficult goal; on the other, however, students may sacrifice academic honors, work experience, and extracurricular and volunteer activities, which contribute to their maturity level and qualifications. Employers usually ask students *what they accomplished* during college, not *how quickly they graduated*. For some students graduating early is a good choice. For others it is not. Early graduation requires trade-offs that students should weigh carefully.

Graduating Late

B. J. said, "My parents told me that I should ask you about the best time to graduate. I'll be a fifth-year senior next fall and will have enough credits to graduate in December, but could take some additional courses and wait for May. I've heard that May is a better time to graduate."

His counselor asked him, "When do you want to graduate?"

"Preferably, never!" responded B. J.

Most students are not quite this candid about their reluctance to end their college years and enter the real world; however, their misgivings are evident. Fear of failure is one reason. They accept media reports of a poor job market and sigh, "What's the point? There are no jobs." Inertia overtakes other students, whose lives have been circumscribed by class schedules for 16 to 17 years of school and college.

Only 53 percent of college students nationwide graduate in four years. (The figure is 48 percent for students in public institutions and 67 percent for those in private schools.) The two primary causes for delays in graduations are limited financial aid, which drives students to combine work and school, and light course loads.

Why Students Graduate Late

Light Course Loads

Students at colleges on the semester system generally need to take an average of 15 credit hours each term (excluding summers) to graduate in four years. Increasingly, students are choosing course loads lighter than 15 hours—at least some semesters—and are graduating later as a result.

There are several reasons for a student's decision to take fewer courses. One is to allow more time for employment. According to a University of Washington study, students who worked fewer than 20 hours per week earned better grades than those who did not work at all. Working more than 20 hours a week, however, often detracted from study time and a student's GPA. This could limit a student's options for selective job opportunities and graduate schools. As an alternative some students drop out of college for one term or more to work and save money for college expenses. This option also results in delayed graduation.

Students may take a light course load in an attempt to increase their GPA, since they have more study time for each class. Although their grades may rise, some academic honors (such as the Dean's List or Phi Beta Kappa) require higher qualifying grades for students taking fewer hours. As a result, some students maintain a good GPA but do not have the academic honors normally associated with it.

Some students take a light course load to fulfill their commitment to demanding extracurricular or volunteer activities. Certain leadership positions, such as student body president or editor of the student newspaper, require nearly as many hours as a full-time job. Students may spend just as much time in volunteer activities, often career related, such as tutoring underprivileged children, political campaigns, and social activism. Varsity sports commonly demand 30 or more hours a week for practice, games, and travel.

Other students start the term with a full class load but drop one or two of their courses. Although there are valid reasons for dropping a class, students often bail out at the first sign of boredom or difficulty. The result, of course, is a light load, which delays graduation and might be awkward to explain to a potential employer reviewing a student's transcript. At some universities courses that are dropped late will appear on the transcript, raising further questions from employers or graduate school admissions officers.

Academic Reasons

Students may find their graduation delayed because admission tests reveal they need remedial course work. Remedial classes do not count toward graduation requirements. In addition, students at some institutions are allowed to repeat courses to make better grades, which could prevent them from graduating on schedule. Transfer students sometimes lose course credits when they enroll in a different institution, which also prolongs their college stay.

Many colleges are experiencing financial difficulties and have chosen to decrease the number of courses they offer. Students may have difficulty obtaining the courses needed for their major or as prerequisites for graduation; their graduation may be delayed until they are able to enroll in the necessary courses.

Your child should look ahead and outline a four-year course plan for his or her desired major. (Although the plan will probably change, it will be a good starting point.) He or she should determine which courses are required, and in which sequence, and try to enroll in them as early as possible. If unable to enroll, your child should consider alternatives: investigating whether the course is offered at a neighboring institution and, if so, whether the credits will transfer; discussing the situation with his or her academic adviser or academic dean to learn if there is any way to enroll in the class; or talking with the class instructor to see if there is some flexibility in the size of the class or if any students have dropped the class since he or she tried to enroll.

As emphasized in Chapter 3, many students change majors several times during their college years. If the former major is very different from the new one—as, for example, with a switch from English to biology—the student may need additional time to complete core courses and related electives. Students may want to consider continuing in the current major and adding a minor or electives in the new area of interest if changing majors will delay graduation. This is especially true if the student is an upperclassman and the new major is not directly career related.

Increasingly more majors, such as accounting, pharmacy, and some engineering disciplines, require five years to complete. Also, universities may either require or strongly encourage students in particular majors, like engineering, to participate in cooperative education programs, generally resulting in an extra semester or two. Students in these programs are not actually graduating late, but they will not, of course, graduate in four years.

Study abroad may also lengthen the time to graduate, since courses taken at a foreign university may not all transfer, and students may miss required courses that are offered only once a year.

Students may receive poor academic advising and not realize that they are missing courses required for graduation. Many colleges provide a checklist to help students ensure that they have the right combination of courses and credit hours necessary to graduate in their major.

Slow Maturation

A survey of parents at the University of North Carolina at Chapel Hill, one of the lower-cost public institutions, revealed that about a quarter of them thought that students "felt no pressure to graduate in four years." Although students would be loath to admit it, many use college as a time to "find themselves." If they don't have a career direction as their senior year approaches, they are fearful of graduating and being at a loss for what to do next. Hence they prolong college by taking "just a few more courses" in hopes of finding a career focus or feeling ready to leave the cocoon of the college environment.

Impact of Graduating Late

Employers sometimes evaluate late graduation negatively. They believe it may reveal a lack of motivation, poor planning, or academic problems. Late graduation is more obvious when a student finishes a degree in December or the summer. A five-year degree may go without notice if the student is graduating in May. However, a student should be prepared with an explanation if interviewers ask about the reasons for late graduation.

Although students may believe they have good reasons to delay graduation, parents are also interested in the economic impact. The "opportunity cost" of graduating late includes tuition and fees, books, and foregone income during any extra terms. Students who take an extra term and graduate in December instead of May or June could lose nearly $20,000 assuming college costs of $5,000 for one additional term and foregone wages of $2,083 for seven months.

Some students assume that parental financial support will last indefinitely. Parents should inform students early if the family budget for education is available for a specific length of time, such as four years.

Best Months to Graduate

According to a survey conducted by the University of North Carolina at Chapel Hill, employers prefer to hire college students who graduate in May and

December. Recruiters ranked June third and August last. Large organizations, such as Fortune 500 corporations or federal government agencies, schedule their management trainee programs to begin when most college students graduate. Students completing their studies "out of sync" may find that they have to wait for the next training program. For an August graduate the delay could be four to five months. Employers may assume that highly qualified students will not remain available and therefore not consider them for employment.

Bottom Line

It is obvious that there is no one answer that is right for all students concerning time to graduate. In many situations involving late graduation, there is little, if any, choice. We suggest that you frequently discuss with your son or daughter his or her academic plans and progress, closely examining the advantages, disadvantages, and likely consequences of each decision. We also recommend consulting with the college's academic and career advisers about these decisions and their impact.

Summary

Graduating Early

Possible Advantages

- Money saved on tuition
- Graduation at younger age
- Earlier graduate/professional school start
- Earlier career/employment start

Possible Disadvantages

- Lower grades
- Fewer opportunities to take electives (either for enhancing marketability or expanding education)

- Less time for summer/part-time work experience, internships, etc.
- Less time for leadership roles, volunteer work
- Less time for personal growth and maturation

Most Appropriate Candidates

- Students with very limited financial support
- Students with excellent grades and who are planning immediately to enter lengthy graduate/professional programs (e.g., medical, dental, veterinary, law school; Ph.D. program)
- Students with good-to-excellent grades planning to enter high-demand careers requiring little experience (e.g., nursing, pharmacy, math or science teaching)

Graduating Late

Possible Advantages

- More time for slow starters to ease into college and improve grades (by taking fewer classes)
- Chance for student to change major rather than graduate in an ill-fitting one
- More time to take extra courses of interest or to improve employability (e.g., electives in business, accounting, or computer science)
- More time to gain career-related work experience through cooperative education, internship programs, or part-time jobs
- More time for extracurricular, volunteer, and leadership activities
- More study time for each course (due to lighter course load), possibly resulting in higher grades

Possible Disadvantages

- Greater college costs
- Many employers and graduate schools prejudiced against students graduating in 4+ years

Most Appropriate Candidates

- Students transferring from other schools or changing majors
- Students in programs where 4+ years for graduation is the norm (e.g., pharmacy, accounting, engineering)
- Students taking lighter course loads to allow time for employment
- Students studying abroad
- Students needing to drop out of school for a term for personal, medical, or academic reasons

Conversation Starters for Parents and Students

1. How long does your major usually require for graduation?
2. How much time does your [extracurricular] activity and volunteer work take per week?
3. Have you considered summer school? Why or why not?
4. What do you think are the disadvantages of your graduating early or graduating late?

CHAPTER 5

GETTING EXPERIENCE AND MAKING CONTACTS

Three Résumés

Kathryn Johnson, a recruiter for a consumer products company, looks at the stack of over a hundred résumés from the university where she will recruit next month for sales representatives. She represents a company that is very selective. Her employer recruits from only 28 universities nationwide, a decrease from 90 schools three years ago.

Ms. Johnson will consider students with any major for these openings, but competitive applicants must have leadership skills, a sincere interest in sales, a high energy level, and a record of setting and achieving goals. They must also be well-rounded team players. Grades are not a major factor, but candidates must have at least a 2.8 GPA, preferably a 3.0. The job pays $30,000 a year to start, and students consider the company to be a prestigious employer. The first three résumés Ms. Johnson reviews reflect the difference in students' backgrounds.

Résumé 1: Brandon

Brandon, an economics major, has a 2.5 GPA. The glee club appears to be his only activity on campus. He held a part-time job for one year shelving books in the library and worked one summer as a lifeguard and another as a waiter.

Résumé 2: Laura

Laura majored in history and minored in Spanish. She has a 2.9 GPA and was on the Dean's List one semester. Her activities include volunteer work as a Big Buddy to an underprivileged child, intramural volleyball, and membership on the social committee for her residence hall. Her résumé cites courses in public speaking, accounting, and marketing.

Laura has spent her last three summers as a sales clerk in a department store, as a camp counselor, and as head camp counselor (a promotion). Part-time jobs as a waitress and as a receptionist helped her earn 40 percent of her college expenses. She lists computer skills such as Word 6.0 and Excel.

Résumé 3: Trent

Trent majored in English and minored in business. His GPA is 3.2, and he has been on the Dean's List three semesters. His résumé states his objective: "A position as a sales representative with opportunities for advancement."

The rest of Trent's résumé is consistent with an interest in sales. One section is labeled "Related Courses" and lists marketing, consumer behavior, and advertising. Another heading is "Related Experience" and lists jobs as a sales associate in a men's clothing store, a sales representative for college telephone directories (in which he sold ad space to businesses), and a promotion to sales team leader for the same firm. He also had a marketing internship with a stockbrokerage firm, where he assisted with a direct mail campaign to identify prospective clients.

Trent also developed his persuasive skills through serving as rush chairman for his fraternity (recruiting new members), as fund-raiser for the university development office (making calls to alumni to solicit donations), and as campaign manager for a student body president candidate. In addition, he is captain of his intramural basketball team. He has extensive computer skills and is proficient in French.

Career Planning and Career Competition

You can see why competition is keen for management trainee positions. If a recruiter sees many résumés like Trent's, other candidates pale in comparison. Trent is representative of students who select a career interest early and do effective career planning.

Like most students, Trent didn't *begin* college with a burning desire to pursue sales as a career. He needed a part-time job, and retail sales positions were easy to find. A friend recruited Trent to join the rush committee of his fraternity. Since he enjoyed both of these activities and was successful in them, Trent decided to look for other opportunities to use his persuasive skills and to target sales as a career.

Laura's résumé goes into the "maybe" pile. It would have been easier for her to compete for job openings several years ago, when entry-level jobs were more plentiful and fewer students obtained career-related experience prior to graduation. Even if her background is not targeted enough for this employer, it may be attractive to retailers and nonprofits.

Ms. Johnson spends little time on Brandon's résumé. There are many students like him. They may have an active social life in college and do not put much effort into their studies. Their families may not expect them to help finance their education and do not make work a priority for their college student. Some students attend summer school or travel during semester breaks and are not available for work. Regardless of the reasons, students like Brandon will find it difficult to obtain interviews with prospective employers.

Students without focus or experience will need to work harder at the job search. Since on-campus interviews are so competitive, they will need to be especially assertive in obtaining interviews off campus (see Chapter 9). After graduation they may need to begin at a low-level position, such as sales clerk or bank teller, to prove themselves first and then apply for promotion from within the organization to a management training program. Another option is to find an unpaid internship after graduation to develop marketable skills and make contacts.

Many students find their niche through trial and error and are still able to develop impressive backgrounds by graduation. Beth entered college as an engineering major but did not find her classes interesting. As a result of her summer job in a manufacturing plant, she became fascinated with the emphasis on self-directed work teams and Total Quality Management. She decided to change her major to business and concentrated in production management. Her engineering background is an asset in this field.

You want your child to have the best possible preparation for his or her future career. This chapter will give some ideas about ways for your son or daughter to obtain career-related experience and marketable skills.

Internships

Marketability to Employers

Large corporations have fewer openings for new college graduates than in the past as a result of downsizing, reorganization, and automation. They can afford to be highly selective. Internships and other career-related experiences are becoming increasingly important. A survey of employers by Michigan State

University reveals that nearly 60 percent of their new hires from college campuses have some relevant experience. According to one employer, "Within three years our goal is for 50 percent of our new hires to come from our previous interns." One Fortune 500 company recently filled *all* of its sales trainee openings with former interns.

It is not unusual for employers to interview students with multiple job-related internships, part-time jobs, and extracurricular or volunteer activities. These candidates have a competitive advantage. Employers are reluctant to take a risk on unfocused, inexperienced students when training and turnover costs are so high. College students used to be hired for their potential. Today they need proven skills. Former interns have been tested, according to recruiters. Internship experience also provides students with polish and business savvy so that they adjust more quickly to a first job after college.

The most competitive employers target students with experience in the same industry. One investment banking recruiter expresses a preference for students with an internship with a national or regional investment bank. Also acceptable, he says, is experience with a major commercial bank, brokerage firm, or Fortune 500 company.

Definition of an Internship

An internship differs from a summer or part-time job in that an internship consists of career-related work rather than such duties as typing, filing, waiting on tables, or operating a cash register. The internship can be compared to an apprenticeship. It may include assisting a professional with day-to-day activities or completing special project assignments. Every intern can expect to perform some clerical or routine duties, but these activities should not constitute the bulk of the student's time.

Students perform internships in industries as diverse as entertainment, stockbrokerage, health care, retailing, law, and government. Examples of internship employers and the positions they offer include *Time* magazine (marketing), Performance Research (sports marketing research), the Spoleto Festival (media relations, orchestra management), and the National Institutes of Health (technology transfer and licensing). Some organizations offer internships abroad. The Center for Austrian Studies sponsors a one-month banking internship in Vienna. A study-abroad program, Internships in Europe, matches students with unpaid internships related to their career interests.

Benefit of Internships

"Reality testing" is an important feature of internships. An internship can provide exposure to a career field, industry, and employer without the pressure of making a long-term commitment. Your child may not have realized that

RÉSUMÉ-BUILDING INTERNSHIPS

What do interns do? You might be surprised at the diversity of their positions and the amount of responsibility they are given. Here are excerpts from the résumés of some students with internship experience.

Planning Intern—Business major

- Taught computer skills to ten managers and planning department professionals; software included Excel, Microsoft Word, Microsoft Mail, and Power Point
- Developed Excel model to quote delivery dates for an experimental product line, using complicated macro and statistical formulas

Film Intern—Radio/TV/Motion Picture major

- Studied film production on the sets of films at Universal Studios, Amblin Entertainment, and Warner Brothers

Brokerage Intern—Business major

- Performed evaluations of postbankruptcy companies, closed-end funds, corporate insider trading, and corporate spin-offs
- Developed computer screens to identify value and growth-oriented stocks using Bloomberg, Factset, and Lotus 1-2-3 software

Computer Support Intern—Mathematical Science major

- Installed, tested and debugged a job hot line (a program that uses voice response technology and synthesized speech)
- Created, updated, and modified databases using FoxPro
- Performed troubleshooting on office software and hardware problems

Congressional Intern—Political Science major

- Studied federal entitlement programs, focusing on means-tested welfare programs and current reform proposals at the state and federal level
- Briefed congressional offices on pending legislation

continued

Newsroom Intern—Journalism/Speech Communication major

- Wrote scripts and edited videos for news feeds to local television affiliates
- Wrote wire stories for the Associated Press
- Listened to scanner for breaking news stories

Industrial Engineering Co-op—Industrial Engineering major

- Analyzed the staffing of materials management departments, and provided data to support elimination of 15 professional positions
- Developed flowchart for the production process of circuit boards to calculate failure rates, determine bottlenecks, and reduce lead times

Health Care Intern—Health Policy/Administration major

- Aided in developing recruitment plan for physical therapy department
- Audited personnel and health files in preparation for accreditation review

Legal Intern—History major

- Located and interrogated witnesses in preparation for trial
- Prepared motions for joinder and supplementary discovery materials
- Assisted district attorney in analyzing strengths and weaknesses of cases

Credit Analyst Intern—Economics major

- Performed annual reviews of credit relationships in excess of $1 million, including risk analysis of repayment capacity
- Calculated and analyzed cash flow coverage

Public Policy Intern—Administration of Criminal Justice major

- Analyzed issues and prepared briefing books for decision makers
- Organized Chamber of Commerce efforts to solicit donations from corporations to benefit local public schools
- Researched family benefits policies; arranged parenting-skills seminars for employees

continued

Engineering Intern—Electrical Engineering major

- Worked with other engineers to develop and test new products
- Prepared engineering studies based on statistical and equipment data

Actuarial Intern—Actuarial Science major

- Created and analyzed management reports for Employee Benefits Division

advertising was so fast-paced. Or, a student may find that human resources involves more than recruiting and training functions, and that salary and benefits administration are not as appealing after first-hand exposure.

The internship experience can enable your child to use and enhance current skills and develop new ones. In some cases, assignments may result in tangible work samples for your child to show prospective employers: for example, full-color graphics for a manager's presentation, or written articles for a company newsletter. An internship will stand out on a senior's résumé, particularly if it is related to a career goal. Since many organizations use internships as a recruiting source, your child is likely to have an "edge" when being considered by the internship employer for a full-time job. The International Foundation, which places sophomores and juniors in benefits administration internships, boasts that 97 percent of its interns receive offers from their sponsoring employers.

An internship can result in a higher salary offer later. A poll by Coopers & Lybrand found that about half of the 187 employers they surveyed offered a salary premium to recent college graduates with work experience such as internships. Your son or daughter's salary offer as a senior may be $100–200 a month higher than for their peers who did not hold an internship. Former interns may also be promoted more quickly as a result of their experience.

Internships can serve as stepping-stones to contacts and future opportunities. Student interns can meet many people in addition to their coworkers: customers or clients, suppliers, and so on. All of these contacts become potential networking connections for job leads. Also, students learn many job search skills while seeking an internship: writing a résumé, preparing cover letters, networking with contacts, completing applications, and interviewing for openings. Former interns have a head start senior year when they look for regular employment.

How do employers benefit by offering internships? They supplement their staff with eager and talented young people who may be considered for future employment. Some interns have learned state-of-the-art techniques on campus and bring new ideas to an organization. Students sometimes make contributions for which they are long remembered. The Federal Reserve Bank of Minneapolis named its electronic bulletin board Kimberley, after a summer intern who designed the system in 1989!

Internship Goal Setting

Your child may say, "I want to find an internship," yet need help in thinking through his or her goals. Goals could include testing an interest in one of several career fields, developing specific skills, and making contacts. For example, a student may wish to explore graphic arts as a career, upgrade skills with computer graphics and desktop publishing software, and develop contacts in Atlanta. The college's career office can help with this goal-setting process.

Next, your child needs to identify the factors to be considered in an internship search. Will he or she need a part-time internship so as to also attend summer school? Does he or she need to earn money, or is an unpaid internship possible? Are there geographic limitations to consider or is relocation or commuting an option? Internships are often difficult to obtain, and your child should be as flexible as possible. Geographic mobility and willingness to accept unpaid internships will increase possible choices.

We can imagine what you are thinking: "But I want my child to return home for the summer." Especially if your son or daughter attends college away from home, you look forward to this time. However, experience in another city may be instrumental in opening future opportunities to work in his or her chosen field after graduation. You may need to sacrifice some of your own needs to help your child make a decision about internship opportunities.

Employers often prize evidence of a student's adaptability. If a position requires travel or relocation, recruiters are sometimes reluctant to hire students who have not worked, traveled, or studied outside their home state. Students from small towns or rural areas may find it especially difficult to compete for openings in large metropolitan areas like New York City or Chicago; employers believe that these candidates may be unable to adjust to such a different environment. A student's internship in a metropolitan area may reassure prospective employers.

Internship Job Search

Once your child determines goals and parameters for the internship, it's time to begin searching for organizations to contact. Your child's career office is likely to maintain resources such as *The National Directory of Internships* and *America's Top 100 Internships* to help identify prospective employers. Because these internships are widely publicized, applicants face heavy competition from the many other students who also have access to the listings. Some students apply to several hundred employers in order to secure an internship.

In addition to printed materials, the career office may have a service through which they mail résumés of students seeking internships to employers who list openings. Some employers also conduct on-campus interviews to recruit interns; however, most students find their positions through more informal methods such as networking.

Internships at some organizations may be targeted for minority students or technical majors. Also, some organizations offer internships and summer jobs to employees' children and rarely offer them to others. As a parent you can check with your employer's human resources department to see whether such opportunities are available. Also, consider possibilities with a family business. Students often assume higher-level responsibilities when they work for a parent, aunt, or brother-in-law.

Students may create their own internships through networking with relatives, friends of the family, neighbors, faculty, and other sources. Initiative and assertiveness can pay off. One accounting student approached a recruiter from a small bank at a college career fair and convinced him that she would be a valuable intern. The recruiter was so impressed with her that he created an internship position for her that she held for two summers. The bank offered her a job when she graduated!

Most formal internship programs target students the summer between their junior and senior years. Freshmen and sophomores usually find their opportunities to obtain internships are limited. They may need to volunteer for part-time internships during the school year and take summer jobs that are less career related but nevertheless allow them to start acquiring skills and building their résumé.

Academic Credit for Internships

Your child should check on his or her college's policy on receiving academic credit for internships. Some schools allow students to be paid for an internship *and* receive credit; others do not permit an intern to receive both. Academic credit requirements for internships are usually demanding. Students may have to prepare a learning contract to specify their learning objectives for the experience. They may also need to keep a journal of their activities, prepare an annotated bibliography (a brief summary of information in the sources) about the field in which they work, and write a paper about their internship. Their supervisor will probably be asked to write a performance evaluation at the conclusion of the internship.

Unpaid Internships

Your son tells you about an ideal internship. It sounds like the perfect opportunity, but you sense that it is almost too good to be true. In the next breath, he mentions that it is unpaid. You are skeptical. Why shouldn't he be paid for his efforts? And shouldn't he help finance his college expenses? If the internship is in another city, your concerns mount. This "opportunity" may actually *cost* you money if you have to pay for housing, food, and commuting costs, which would be minimal if he lived at home.

On the other hand, you realize that this type of internship may not be available in your city (for example, publishing or film work). You son could spend another summer working at the yogurt shop, but that will not increase his chances to work in his field when he graduates.

There is a way to compromise. Some students work by day in an unpaid internship and work at night or on weekends for pay. As an alternative they may decide to work more hours at a paid job during the school year to compensate for their loss of income during the summer.

Internships for College Graduates

Some employers will consider new college graduates for internship openings. These positions are often unpaid, but they provide an opportunity for graduates to acquire marketable skills. Once interns prove their worth, they may be offered paid employment. Even if they do not receive a job offer, interns will gain experience and contacts, which often increase their chances of finding a paid position.

Externships

Many people who are familiar with the concept of internships may not have heard of *externships*. A student who is considering a particular occupation, such as banking, may find it helpful to observe someone on the job in that field. This short-term experience is called an externship, or job shadowing.

An externship experience usually lasts from half-a-day to a week. Semester breaks are ideal for students to participate in externships. The career office may match students with alumni or other contacts for externships. Students may also arrange for this experience on their own through personal or information interview contacts. Although an externship often does not provide hands-on experience, it can be beneficial. Your child can observe many characteristics of a possible career field. An extern may seek answers to the following questions:

- What are the duties of the job?

- Is the pace high pressure or relaxed?

- Does the job involve heavy contact with other people, or is the work more solitary?

- Does the person in the job work regular hours or frequent overtime?

- Would I feel comfortable with the personalities of people in this job or department? Would I fit in?

- What is the environment like? Do people wear traditional business dress such as suits, or are they casually dressed? Is the workplace plushly decorated or austere?

Your son or daughter may decide after an externship that an occupation is not a good match after all and be spared a dissatisfying first job after college. A positive experience could reinforce a career interest and provide contacts for a future internship.

Students often mention externship experiences during job interviews and on graduate school applications as evidence of serious interest in a career field. Recruiters have said that they are impressed with students who have completed an internship, an externship, or an informational interview in the field for which they are applying. These applicants are more likely to have realistic expectations about the career and know whether they will enjoy it and perform well in it.

Self-Employment

Some students create their own opportunities for work experience though self-employment:

- They design, order, and sell T-shirts with unique slogans.

- They operate a lawn care or house-painting service.

- They provide roommate-matching services for students in apartments.

- They use desktop publishing software as part of laying out and distributing customer newsletters for small businesses.

- They tutor students.

- They sell soft drinks and sandwiches at the beach during school breaks.

Student entrepreneurs develop many skills, such as advertising and selling a product or service, negotiating or setting prices, ensuring customer satisfaction, ordering inventory or scheduling services, keeping records, and filing taxes. Many also recruit and supervise other students, developing leadership skills.

Employers are often impressed with the initiative, risk taking, and work ethic of self-employed students, but too much entrepreneurial activity may raise a red flag. A recruiter may wonder whether a student can take direction as an employee. A recruiter may also be cautious about hiring a budding entrepreneur for a lengthy training program, in case the student's hidden agenda is future self-employment. Student entrepreneurs should plan to obtain experience as an employee in addition to working for themselves.

Students may obtain entrepreneurial experience on some campuses. Columbia Student Enterprises at Columbia University includes a messenger service, tutoring, a deli, and charter bus service, among other services.

Door-to-Door Sales

Many parents are alarmed to hear about their child's plans to spend the summer selling books (or other merchandise) door-to-door in a strange city on a commission basis. This opportunity may be labeled as an internship. Students are usually recruited by other students, who would supervise them as part of a sales team. A would-be recruit is regaled with examples of students with very high earnings (as much as $10,000–45,000 in a summer).

What is the real story? It is true that some students earn over $10,000 in three months, usually as "student managers" in their second or third summer with the company. They profit from their own sales as well as from the sales of their team members. These star performers give testimonials about large profits, exciting incentive trips, and personal rewards that resulted from their experience.

Successful students rave about their summers selling door-to-door. They speak of the experience as one that led to their increased confidence, self-discipline, and interpersonal skills. In addition, these students say that they are proud of running their own business (as an independent contractor) and living independently.

Students who have sold books, for example, earn an average of $5,640 during their first summer, according to one publisher. But this figure does not include students who drop out early (about one in five). Many students experience homesickness, become disillusioned with selling, or tire of 80-hour work weeks. (Students are encouraged to make a sales presentation to a prescribed number of prospects a day, and they receive a special award for putting in exceptionally long hours.)

Parents are often skeptical about door-to-door sales. Many call the college career office with questions:

How safe is door-to-door sales?
   Students are typically assigned to rural or suburban locations. Employers give them guidelines for determining how to approach sales prospects. Female students are usually cautioned not to enter a home with a man unless he is accompanied by his wife or children.

How will my child find a place to live in another state?
   One company provides a list of local families willing to rent rooms to college students and a list of churches with other referrals.

Can my child sell enough to cover expenses and make any profit?

Some students find this experience very lucrative; however, it is possible for students to *lose* money if they do not keep their living expenses low and work enough hours. Those who quit may find it hard to find other work because summer positions are filled by that time.

How do prospective employers evaluate this experience?

Some employers (especially those recruiting for sales representatives) actually *ask* career offices for a list of students who spent a summer selling books door-to-door for a particular publisher. Others are favorably impressed with the experience when they see it on a résumé. Recruiters state that these students are self-motivated, confident, and mature and have already proven themselves to have unusual perseverance.

If your child is interested in fields that are very difficult to enter, such as journalism, broadcasting, or investment banking, directly related experience would be more helpful than door-to-door sales.

What kind of training is provided?

Students receive training in sales techniques and product knowledge. Some employers provide excellent training—as much as a full week—which can give students useful skills.

Door-to-door sales is a lucrative, character-building experience for some students and a big disappointment for others. Your child should explore all the facts before making a decision. You can help by suggesting questions to ask about this type of opportunity (such as the ones listed above). Your child should also request a list of students who sold for the company the previous summer and contact them for further information.

Other commission opportunities include selling cutlery or fire extinguishers, and painting houses. Students sell cutlery or fire extinguishers in their hometown, making sales demonstrations to friends and relatives and asking for referrals to contact. Paint-contracting companies recruit students to solicit business painting residential houses; some of these students supervise others and gain leadership experience.

Most parents do not consider these independent contractor positions to pose as much risk as door-to-door sales in another state. However, all straight commission positions carry some risks, since they do not provide any guaranteed income; compensation is based on a percentage of sales.

The Invisible Curriculum

Importance to Employers

In a College Placement Council Foundation survey employers responded that they considered students' personal traits and skills more important to success on the job than their "domain knowledge" (knowledge related to their major). Some of these personal traits included adaptability, risk taking, and creativity; the skills included problem solving, teamwork, decision making, and oral and written communication.

Many employer interview questions probe for these personal traits and skills. A recruiter may say to a student, "Give me an example of a time you solved a difficult problem." Another question could be, "Tell me a story about a time you took a risk and failed at a project. What did you learn from this experience?"

Employers with management training programs typically target students whose résumés show active involvement in campus student organizations. Students in these groups frequently encounter situations that require teamwork, conflict resolution, and other useful skills.

Employers are especially interested in students who have leadership roles, which serve as a "proxy" for supervisory experience and help employers identify applicants with management potential. Most students have not had the opportunity to supervise others in a work setting, or their supervisory experience is limited to nonbusiness settings in positions such as head lifeguard, head waitress, or senior camp counselor.

Extracurricular Activities as Experience

Extracurricular activities sometimes provide students with even more powerful skills than internships. Consider these examples, excerpted from students' résumés:

President, Student Union
- Chaired the Board of Directors, which controls a $450,000 annual budget for programming films, art exhibits, concerts, speakers, festivals, and other special events

Co-Chair, Student Symposium
- Planned and organized a two-day event for over 700 students, faculty, and executives

- Coordinated facilities and catering of three meals for all participants

- Supervised 85 volunteers on the Facilities Committee

As indicated in Chapter 1, campus organizations are diverse, and students develop many skills through leadership roles. Students at large universities have literally hundreds of organizations from which to choose, such as student government; sororities, fraternities, and residence halls; sports teams; clubs for individual majors; professional associations; political and religious groups; community service organizations; and cultural groups.

If you have a daughter who is a future banker or financial management trainee, she may want to run for treasurer in a club, student professional organization, or sorority. Many student treasurers administer budgets that exceed $100,000.

If you have a son who is a would-be advertising, marketing, or fund-raising professional, he will find many leadership positions or committees related to his career goals. He can serve as a chairperson or member of a publicity, fraternity rush (recruiting), or philanthropy (fund-raising) committee. If he aspires to a career in college admissions, he can help recruit prospective students to campus. He can serve a tour guide for high school students and their parents.

A budding performer or writer does not necessarily have to be a drama or music major to audition for plays and choral groups. Campuses often have student-run television stations, radio stations, newspapers, literary journals, and publications devoted to political or social commentary.

Is your child interested in a career in law? Many campuses have a student-administered honor code. Students serve as defense attorneys, prosecutors, and jury members for hearings in which peers are accused of cheating, plagiarism, or other offenses. This experience provides students with research, interviewing, and public speaking skills. Some campuses or college towns offer a mediation or dispute settlement center and train students as mediators. Prospective lawyers also frequently participate in student government.

A student who is interested in international work can volunteer as an English conversation partner for a foreign student or enroll in a study-abroad program. Some students volunteer to translate for hospital patients who do not speak English. Others seek part-time or summer jobs at import or export firms.

"Promotions" in Campus Organizations

Students learn about teamwork and organizational behavior through their campus involvement. In addition, they can be "promoted" to positions of more responsibility. Here is a résumé excerpt that illustrates a student's progression from freshman to senior:

Delta Delta Delta Sorority

Treasurer of Pledge Class (Freshman year)
- Collected and accounted for $2,500 raised for charity by pledge class

Assistant Treasurer (Sophomore year)
- Managed individual member activities accounts

Treasurer (Junior year)
- Coordinated membership dues payments
- Collected past due accounts

Vice President of Finance (Senior year)
- Plan and implement $500,000 budget
- Maintain accountability of sorority's fiscal status
- Supervise and train treasurer

The next example shows how another student learns to "pay his dues" before assuming more responsibility:

THE EXPONENT (a student newspaper with daily circulation of 35,000)

Staff Writer (Freshman year)
- Wrote stories for University Desk. Covered student body president election and other general assignments

Assistant Managing Editor (Sophomore year)
- Laid out inside pages, pasted up paper, supervised production of one-shot business supplement

Editorial Writer (Junior year)
- Wrote two weekly editorials and a humor column

Associate Editor (Senior year)
- Write two weekly editorials, edit letters and columns, solicit artwork, supervise writers, lay out and paste up pages

---

The following box display provides examples of campus activities and volunteer work as they relate to marketable skills.

Sports Activities

Employers associate many positive characteristics with students' participation in sports. These students are often assumed to have a high energy level and to be competitive, goal oriented, and disciplined. Employers may have seen games in which athletes perform under pressure—as a whole stadium watches! In addition, many athletes receive valuable experience in public speaking as a result of media interviews. Team sports yield additional benefits as students learn teamwork skills.

Varsity sports may require long hours for training, travel, and competition. Employers usually take this into consideration when weighing a student athlete's grades and experience.

Your child doesn't need to be a varsity athlete to list sports activities on a résumé. Many employers also favorably evaluate involvement with intramural and club sports.

Religious, Political, and Minority Organizations

Some campus or volunteer activities may be controversial, and students should seek advice before including them on a résumé (e.g., pro-life or pro-choice

EXTRACURRICULAR AND VOLUNTEER EXPERIENCE:
Résumé Excerpts Showing Marketable Skills

Leadership Skills

Student Attorney General—Judiciary Branch, Student Government
- Administered honor code for student body of 16,000 students
- Investigated over 100 honor code violations (cheating, plagiarism, etc.)
- Selected, trained, and managed 40 staff members and 7 associates

Resident Assistant—College Residence Hall
- Enforced housing policies and regulations for 60 residents
- Planned and implemented social and educational programs for students
- Served as team leader for interviewing R.A. applicants

Captain and Coach—Rugby Club
- Coached undefeated 1996 season, winning state championship
- Voted Most Valuable Player for 1996 season

Group Commander—Air Force ROTC
- Supervised 80 cadets (freshmen–seniors)
- Conducted leadership training and evaluated cadet performance
- Served as president of Promotion Board

Marketing Skills

Fund-raiser—College Development Office
- Made cold calls to alumni to solicit donations
- Raised over $8,000 in 13 weeks
- Ranked in the top ten percent of callers

Volunteer Coordinator—Senate Campaign
- Recruited and supervised college student volunteers
- Assisted with "Get out the Vote" initiative
- Trained callers to conduct telephone survey of voters

Account Executive—Student Newspaper
- Sold display advertising in a geographic territory
- Prospected for new clients; serviced 50 regular clients
- Assisted clients to create advertisements and campaigns

continued

Quantitative Skills

Treasurer—Fraternity
- Administered and allocated $414,000 annual budget
- Managed accounts payable and receivable for over 170 members
- Served on Executive Council and chaired Finance Committee

Tutor—Service Organization
- Tutored high school students in beginning and intermediate algebra and calculus

Communication Skills

Reporter—Student Newspaper
- Wrote feature stores for special tabloids
- Reported current events for city and state

Volunteer Writer—Nonprofit Agency
- Wrote press releases and public service announcements
- Researched and wrote articles for two quarterly newsletters and annual report

Volunteer—Crisis Hot Line
- Completed 50 hours of crisis intervention training
- Responded to callers with concerns such as unplanned pregnancy, domestic violence, and depression
- Provided callers with referrals to social service agencies

Research Assistant—Psychology Department
- Tested subjects in study on depression in women

Computer Skills

Computer Lab Assistant—Computer Science Department
- Provided programming and technical instruction for students
- Evaluated the quality of lab assignments

Student Software Engineer—Computer Science Department
- Designed and implemented a graphical user interface for biological sequence analysis hardware as part of a four-person team

continued

- Programmed in UNIX C
- Wrote parts of project plan, user manual, and implementation manual

Foreign Language Skills

Japanese Tutor—Self-Employed
- Tutored juniors and seniors in advanced-level Japanese

Volunteer Translator—University Medical Center
- Translated for Spanish-speaking patients

abortion activities). Students may also want to avoid listing organizations that identify them by political party, religion, or ethnicity. On the other hand, many employers strive for diversity in their workforce, so this information could serve to positively differentiate a student.

Your child should avoid limiting his or her extracurricular involvement and employment to organizations that may seem one-dimensional or indicate a lack of ability to work with diverse populations. One student's résumé included these entries: worked on a kibbutz in Israel, taught Hebrew at a synagogue school, and volunteered with B'nai B'rith. She later expressed regret that her résumé lacked breadth. Another student majored in Afro-American studies, served as vice president of the NAACP student chapter, chaired the publicity committee of the Black Cultural Center, and volunteered to tutor minority children. He developed good leadership skills but remarked that he wished his résumé reflected his wide-ranging interests more effectively.

Employers sometimes ask questions to determine whether students have worked in organizations with members from different racial and cultural backgrounds. Regardless of your child's ethnicity, he or she should plan some involvement (campus activities, courses, or work experience) that demonstrates this exposure.

High School Burnout

Your child may decide as a freshman that he or she is burned out from student activities in high school, reasoning, "Since I have already proven my leadership ability to myself and others, why is it necessary to become so involved at college?" You may want to caution your child about the consequences of this approach.

Employers are likely to view high school accomplishments as ancient history. In fact, high school experiences do not belong on a college senior's résumé. (They may be included on résumés of freshmen, sophomores, and juniors when applying for internships.) Also, leadership roles in college present higher-level challenges, since student officers may interact with faculty, alumni, senior campus administrators, and others.

Although extracurricular involvement is worthwhile, freshmen should begin with a modest time commitment. Their first priority should be establishing a good academic record.

The Double Agenda

Just as your child should take a strategic approach to choosing employment and campus activities, he or she should be forward-thinking with class assignments, so they also serve career goals. A professor may allow students to choose their own topic for an essay or speech. How can students tailor this type of assignment to their career interests?

A prospective banking trainee may give a class talk arguing for changes in banking regulations to allow cross-selling of financial services (such as stocks, bonds, and mutual funds). Another student, interested in nonprofit organizations that target social justice issues, may write an essay espousing abolition of capital punishment. An engineering major may write a paper analyzing the differences between civil and environmental engineering as a career path.

Students may also have discretion in choosing topics for an honors thesis or for an independent study project. For example, a student may decide to conduct a market research study of customer satisfaction in the airline industry. Employers are impressed when they learn that a student chose a subject that is relevant to a career interest.

Although many employers will consider students in any major for certain management trainee positions, an interviewer may wonder whether a history major, for example, is sincerely interested in business. Some recruiters are wary of applicants who appear to be just "shopping" or interviewing for practice. A student who has taken some business or economics electives and written a research paper on Total Quality Management, for example, may be a more credible candidate.

Some courses include an experiential component that helps students develop marketable skills. Business students are sometimes given a consulting assignment with a small business. They collect information about a specific problem and make recommendations to resolve it. Students in certain psychology courses are required to perform related volunteer work. Alicia volunteered at a nursing home for three hours a week to satisfy a requirement for her "Psychology of Aging" class. As a result of her natural rapport with this population, she later targeted a job in gerontology and became the activities coordinator for a retirement center. ROTC students assume various positions of responsibility in the cadet corps and participate in a leadership lab.

Students in some fields gain experience through competitive events, such as the Annual International Collegiate Programming Contest, which awards $15,000 in scholarships to winning software programmers. (Microsoft sent recruiters to this event to scout prospects!) Some Purdue University landscape architecture students spend over 300 hours on a design competition judged by professionals in their field. Business students may compete in business case competitions with those from other universities.

Show and Tell

In some fields employers will ask students to provide a portfolio, writing samples, or other examples of their work. Advance planning will ensure that your child has appropriate samples to furnish. One employer reported that a student submitted a very personal diary entry as a writing sample! Here are some examples of career fields in which a portfolio may be necessary:

Consulting—An employer may request a writing sample, usually a class assignment of at least three to five pages, as an example of research, writing, and analytic skills. Students should keep the best examples of their work.

Journalism—Newspapers typically ask applicants to bring clippings to their job interviews. Examples could include articles written for a student newspaper, literary magazine, or other publication. A student can also apply to become a stringer for a local or national publication while in college, which will result in work samples as well as experience. Internships are another source of material, since student interns may write newsletter articles, press releases, and so on.

Art/Graphic design/Advertising—Employers in the arts or communications expect students to prepare a portfolio of their drawings, photography, or other work.

Technical writing—Applicants in this field collect samples of their work, such as instruction manuals, user guides, or articles about technical subjects. Ideal sources include assignments for a technical writing class or materials produced for an employer.

Broadcasting and film—Employers in the media often request students to provide tapes of their work. Students may have obtained these tapes from experience with a student radio or television station, an internship, or a part-time job. In addition, students may make a tape specifically for consideration by prospective employers.

Some education majors have also begun to prepare portfolios for prospective employers. These portfolios may include a student's sample syllabus or lesson plan, a videotape of student teaching, and pictures of bulletin boards or field trips.

Developing Relationships

College seniors are often stumped when asked to provide references on a job application or graduate school admission form. Students realize too late that they have not established close enough contacts with faculty members and other professionals. Since faint praise is almost as bad as a negative reference, students should be confident of a strong recommendation before requesting one.

It may not be easy for students to develop a relationship with professors at a large university, particularly during their freshman or sophomore year. How can a faculty member get to know individual students in an auditorium-sized classroom? A student can enroll in several classes that are taught by the same professor. In addition, a student can participate actively in class discussions and visit the professor during posted office hours to clarify difficult lecture points. Some students work for faculty as graders or research assistants. For students who take the initiative, faculty may become mentors and can be valuable sources of professional contacts for internships and job leads.

Academic advisers and other college administrators may be important contacts. They may oversee a club or other organization in which your son or daughter is active. These professionals may be in the best position to describe your child's leadership skills in a reference letter.

Faculty and administrators are also frequently asked to nominate students for special awards, honoraries, and fellowships.

Making Contacts

In addition to meeting career-related contacts through internships and information interviews, students should identify and join professional associations in their field. Many of these associations charter student chapters on campuses including Alpha Chi Sigma (professional chemistry fraternity), the American Advertising Federation, the American Chemical Society, and the Society of Professional Journalists.

Students at Purdue University may join a Women in Aviation chapter. The organization has hosted speakers such as an airline pilot for United Airlines and a logistics engineer who helps design planes for McDonnell Douglas. Members receive additional exposure to career options at the three-day national conference of the parent organization, Women in Aviation International.

As stressed in Chapter 3, eligible students should join academic honoraries of their major. For example, Psi Chi is the honorary for psychology majors; Delta Phi Alpha, the German honorary society; Beta Gamma Sigma, the honorary for business students. Professionals sometimes interact with these student groups and may be a source of career information, internships, and job leads. Some of these groups sponsor scholarships for members.

Students may also want to join a preprofessional club on their campus, such as the Pre-Law Club or Pre-Vet Club. These clubs usually invite guest speakers such as graduate school admissions officers or professionals who discuss their occupations.

The college alumni association and the student affiliate group also can help your student make valuable contacts. These groups may arrange externships for students and offer other opportunities for them to meet alumni.

Some professionals make presentations in the classroom, participate in special events (such as a symposium or lecture series), and attend career fairs or panels on college campuses. Assertive students increase their visibility by asking good questions, helping to coordinate these activities, or following up later with a thank-you letter.

Student Contributions toward College Expenses

Many employers ask students how they financed their college education in order to determine the student's work ethic and sense of responsibility. "How many hours a week did you work during the school year?" "How many hours a week did you work during the summer?" "What percentage of your college expenses did you personally furnish? How much did you provide through work, loans, and scholarships?"

Some employers are favorably impressed with students who contribute a high proportion of their college expenses; however, students who work long hours (more than 20 hours per week) are less likely to have high grades, related experience (particularly internships), and leadership positions in campus organizations. If students have pressing financial needs, they should consider a combination of part-time work and loans in order to allow sufficient time for study *and* extracurricular activities.

Employers are often favorably impressed by honors such as merit-based financial awards, but a student with a full scholarship should still plan to obtain career-related experience.

Summary

Definition of an Internship

- A career-related experience, similar to an apprenticeship, that commonly lasts a semester, summer, or school year. It may be paid or unpaid, part-time or full-time. Institutions may grant academic credit for internship experience.

Benefits of an Internship

- Exposure to a career field, industry, and employer without a commitment
- Opportunity to use and enhance marketable skills and develop new ones
- An advantage when applying for regular full-time work with the same employer
- A possible salary premium if offered a regular job with the same employer
- Contacts that may be useful for a job search
- Development of job search skills before senior year
- Useful career experience (from both paid and unpaid internships)

Definition of an Externship

- A "job-shadowing" experience to observe a professional, usually for a length of time ranging from half a day to a week.

Benefits of an Externship

- Observation of activities in an occupation or industry which may help a student determine whether to pursue it further
- Contacts that may lead to part-time, internship, or regular job leads

Benefits of Self-Employment

- Development of skills and self-confidence
- Evidence of initiative, perseverance, and resourcefulness for prospective employers

Benefits of Extracurricular Activities

- Development of leadership, teamwork, and other skills

Portfolios of Student Work

- Work samples requested by employers in some fields (for example, consulting, journalism, technical writing)

Benefits of Relationships with Faculty And Administrators

- Identification of mentors
- Possible future references

Benefits of Alumni Club and Professional Association Contacts

- Visibility to professionals in targeted career field

Conversation Starters for Parents and Students

1. What types of internships are available for someone in your field?

2. What campus clubs or activities are you interested in? Which organizations, committees, and offices are related to your career interests?

3. What are some ways you could develop samples of your work to show prospective employers?

4. Which of your faculty or administrators do you think might be able to serve as references for internships (or full-time jobs later)? How will you develop a relationship with them?

CHAPTER 6

"I THINK I'LL GO TO GRAD SCHOOL"

The Thomas family was gathered for Thanksgiving dinner and listened as Nicole, a college senior, described a homecoming party. Her grandmother asked the question on everyone's mind: "What are your plans after graduation?" After a brief pause, Nicole replied, "I plan to go to law school."

At first there was no reaction as family members were caught up in their own thoughts. Nicole's mother looked surprised. ("This is the first I've heard she was interested in law school.") Aunt Janet appeared concerned. ("I wonder how John and his wife will pay for this—they struggled to put her through four years at a private college.") Nicole's cousin tried to conceal his skepticism. ("With her grades? Not a chance!")

Nicole's grandmother broke the silence. "Where are you planning to go to law school?"

"Oh, I don't know. I just decided to go," Nicole hedged.

"How did you do on the LSAT?" Her cousin probed for more information.

"Oh, I haven't taken it yet." Nicole's plan seemed to unravel. Maybe she hadn't given it enough thought. Was there still time to apply?

Many students plan to continue their education for the wrong reasons. Help your son or daughter examine his or her motivation to attend graduate or professional school. Urge caution if you see these signs:

Lack of focus—Is your child uncertain about a career direction and hoping to find it in graduate school? He or she may be still without focus two years (and $30,000) later. This is an expensive route for self-discovery and one that does not always work!

Pressure from others—Does it seem that all of your child's friends are continuing their education? Some students find it difficult to be objective about decision making when others—peers, family members, or faculty—offer their advice. Be sure your child seeks counsel from knowledgeable sources.

Misconceptions about the job market—Some students make the assumption that they cannot get too much education. They believe that a bachelor's degree is devalued today, "as common as a high school diploma used to be." Another misconception is that graduate training guarantees a higher starting salary. Recipients of some graduate and professional degrees do earn high incomes. However, those with a master's in social work, education, divinity, and many liberal arts fields actually earn *less* than many bachelor's degree recipients.

Immaturity—Few students look forward to the job search process. They are often anxious and fear rejection. Some students delay the inevitable by taking refuge in graduate or professional school.

Unrealistic expectations about graduate school—Further education is not simply more of the same undergraduate experience. Graduate students do not have much time for football games, parties, and other social activities, as they face 60- to 80-hour weeks of study and research.

Career Goal as Starting Point

Felicia, a second-year graduate student in speech communication, made an appointment to see her college counselor. "I've decided that I want to change direction. Human resources sounds interesting. How do I qualify for those positions?"

Ironically, a bachelor's graduate with related internships and courses may be more marketable to employers than someone with an unrelated master's degree. If an organization wants to recruit graduate-level human resources candidates, it would most likely target students with an M.S. in human resources or an MBA with a concentration in personnel management. Also, Felicia faces the likely interview question, "Why did you study speech communication if you want to work in human resources?"

A young person who starts with a career focus first and researches its educational requirements is less likely to enroll in a graduate program that is not necessary for his or her field or that will award an inappropriate degree. (Of course, some students may choose to continue their education for the sheer joy of learning without regard to the marketability of their advanced degree.)

Professional schools, such as those in law, medicine, and business, provide practical career training, while graduate degrees such as a Ph.D. or master's tend to be more academic in nature, emphasizing research skills. (See Table 6.1 for examples of graduate degree programs, their duration, projected job growth for degree recipients, and average starting salaries.)

Graduate school advisers wryly comment that, "In graduate school you learn more and more about less and less." One Ph.D. student was asked about his area of research. He responded, "Medieval Italian organ music."

Because graduate study is so specialized, students need to carefully select a career direction prior to enrolling. Is an advanced degree necessary to enter the field? Is a master's or doctoral degree recommended for advancement? If so, do employers prefer applicants who also have full-time work experience? For example, students admitted to the top MBA schools have worked an average of four to five years.

Choosing a graduate school is difficult if a student is not focused. Your daughter may excel in science and want to help people. She could apply to M.D. programs. Other alternatives include a master of science in genetic counseling, a master's in health administration, a master of science in exercise physiology, or a master's in public health. Or, your son may want to attend graduate school in education. Will he pursue an M.A. in teaching English as a second language, or in special education, educational computing, or education administration? An engineering major could obtain an M.S. in biological and irrigation engineering, nuclear engineering, or engineering management, among others.

Graduate School Advisers

Most colleges and universities offer graduate school advising services. Advisers may include administrators and faculty with expertise in one or more areas (such as law school or medical school). If your child is considering graduate or professional school, encourage him or her to consult an adviser as early as possible, ideally by the sophomore year. The health professions, for example, require many prerequisites that must be taken in sequence, and some graduate schools in the humanities and social sciences (e.g., history and psychology) require proficiency in two foreign languages.

Here are some questions for your son or daughter to ask an adviser:

- Which prerequisites are necessary for graduate school admission?

- Which additional courses do you recommend to improve my chances of acceptance?

Table 6.1

GRADUATE AND PROFESSIONAL DEGREES (EXAMPLES)

Degree Name	Degree Abbreviation	Field	Length of Full-Time Study	Job Growth	Typical Starting Compensation
Doctor of Jurisprudence	JD	Law	3 years	↗	$44,149
Doctor of Medicine	MD	Medicine	4 years plus residency	↗	$30,753 (First-year residents) $143,600 (Physicians under age 36)
Master of Business Administration	MBA	Business	1–2 years	Depends on position	$58,369 (Nontechnical bachelor's and 2–4 years experience)
Master of Social Work	MSW	Social work	2 years	↗	$25,000
Doctor of Dental Surgery	DDS	Dentistry	3–4 years	→	$50,000 (Primary private practice—less than 5 years experience)
Doctor of Philosophy	PhD	Various academic disciplines	4–8 years	Depends on discipline	$25,820–47,390 (Assistant professors)
Doctor of Veterinary Medicine	DVM	Veterinary	4 years	↗	$30,694 (Private Practice)

Sources: National Association for Law Placement, Association of American Medical Colleges, American Medical Association—Center for Health Policy Research, National Association of Colleges and Employers, National Association of Social Workers, American Dental Association, American Association of University Professors, Journal of the American Veterinary Medical Association.

- Which extracurricular activities will help me develop relevant skills and be evaluated positively by admissions officers?

- Which work-related or volunteer experiences would enhance my credentials?

- Have alumni been especially successful at applying to particular graduate schools? Which schools?

- What qualifications do I need to be competitive?

- Do you have a timeline to suggest for the application process? For example, when should I register to take the graduate admissions test?

Many health professions advisers, for example, have prepared lists of specific courses recommended for students interested in medicine, dentistry, veterinary medicine, and other programs. Medical school advisers strongly encourage students to take the MCAT in the spring of their junior year. Law school advisers typically recommend a broad education for pre-law students, who may take the LSAT during fall of their senior year.

Table 6.2

ADMISSIONS TESTS

Program	Test Required for Application
Professional Schools	
Dentistry	Dental Admission Testing (DAT)
Medicine	Medical College Admission Test (MCAT)
Optometry	Optometry Admission Test (OAT)
Pharmacy	Pharmacy College Admission Test (PCAT)
Veterinary medicine	Veterinary College Admission Test (VCAT)/ GRE/MCAT
Law	Law School Admission Test (LSAT)
Business	Graduate Management Admission Test (GMAT)
Graduate Schools	
Education	Praxis Series Tests
PhD or MA/MS programs	Graduate Record Examinations (GRE)

Your child may want to request that admissions test scores be sent to his or her undergraduate adviser for use in the counseling process.

Researching and Evaluating Schools

You probably have a certain sense of déjà vu as you watch your child consider graduate or professional schools. Didn't you do this just recently with regard to researching and visiting four-year colleges? In some ways the process is the same. Your child will weigh factors such as reputation of faculty, selectivity, cost, availability of financial aid, and location. He or she should apply to some schools that seem *too* selective for his or her credentials ("reach" schools), others that are a close match, and several that are "safe."

The stakes are higher as your child evaluates the quality of an institution's graduate education. Is the program accredited by the American Assembly of Collegiate Schools of Business (MBA schools), the American Bar Association (law schools), the American Psychological Association (doctoral programs in psychology), or whatever organization might be relevant?

Your child should obtain a catalog for each program he or she is considering. Additional research through books such as *Peterson's Guides* or through the Internet might help. Some electronic sources of graduate school information include Peterson's Guide (http://www.petersons.com), JOBTRAK (http://www.jobtrak.com:80/), and Catapult (http://www.jobweb.org/catapult/catapult.htm).

Students may speak with representatives of many business and law schools at "MBA forums" and "law forums" in major cities. These events also provide general information on admissions, financial aid, and career options. Your child should check with the career office for dates and locations.

A student who graduates from a law school that is accredited by the American Bar Association may take the bar exam in any state. This privilege is not extended to graduates of nonaccredited schools. Only 271 of the 800 MBA schools are accredited by the AACSB, a distinction that may be noted by prospective employers.

Another consideration is the percentage of a school's graduates who pass professional examinations such as the bar (law) or boards (medical fields). Your child should ask, too, about the number of students who obtain related summer internships or employment following graduation.

It is possible that your child will be accepted by a mediocre graduate or professional school that is willing to take his or her tuition money despite a poor academic record. Graduates from undistinguished programs, however, usually do not fare well in a competitive job market—even with the added degree.

Attending a foreign graduate or professional school is an option to consider; however, students may have difficulty obtaining employment in the United States after completion of their studies. Recipients of medical degrees from foreign or offshore programs tend to have a lower pass rate on the national licensure exam and are generally not as competitive for the most desirable residency programs.

Corporations often target graduates of leading business schools in the United States and may be unfamiliar with universities abroad. Some foreign institutions, such as the London School of Economics, are very impressive, though. Your child should consult faculty members and professionals in his or her field for advice about the reputation of graduate degree programs in other countries.

Joint Degree Programs

Some universities offer students the opportunity to graduate with two degrees simultaneously, such as law (J.D.) and MBA. These dual degrees generally require additional time. Students often ask college advisers about joint degree programs. Unfortunately, probing often reveals that these students are unfocused about their career goals. They are interested in attending graduate school: law, business, history, something! By enrolling in a combined program they hope to increase their chances of getting it right.

Combined-degree programs are a good choice for students who have a specialized or interdisciplinary career goal (see Table 6.3). For example, a prospective physician-scientist may seek an M.D. and a Ph.D. in one of the basic sciences, such as molecular biology, neuroscience, immunology, or genetics.

Diane L. Gottheil, coeditor of *The Education of Physician Scholars*, reports that graduates with an M.D.-Ph.D. are very marketable and receive priority consideration for residencies in first-rate research-oriented medical schools. These physicians perform cutting-edge research in fields such as medical imaging and gene transfer. Another attractive credential for M.D.'s is the MBA degree. Executive search firms report that physician-MBAs are in demand as executives to run hospitals and HMOs.

Many other combined-degree programs are available. They are identified in *Peterson's Guides* and in graduate school catalogs. Your child should ask the career services staff of the graduate or professional schools in which they are interested about the number of employers requesting students with dual enrollment and whether these applicants receive higher starting salaries. In many cases, such as with J.D.-MBA programs, the answer may be, "I can't remember the last time any recruiters asked for students with the joint degree. These students do not seem to receive higher salaries than those with one degree."

Students interested in joint degrees need to identify universities with dual

---

Table 6.3

JOINT DEGREE PROGRAMS (EXAMPLES)

Joint Degree	Possible Career Path
JD-PhD (e.g., Bioengineering or Biophysics)	Patent law (e.g., in biotechnology industry)
JD-MBA	Corporate law
JD-PhD in Psychology	Child custody, Divorce mediation, Personal injury, Insanity defense cases
JD-MD	Medical malpractice law
MD-PhD (e.g., Molecular biology or Immunology)	Medical research, Academic medicine
MD-MBA/MHA	Management of hospital or HMO
MBA-PhD in Psychology	Mental health administration

---

degree programs and apply separately to each program (e.g., business and law schools for a J.D.-MBA). An applicant will be accepted or rejected independently by each admissions office.

Enrollment in a combined program will usually shorten the time required to complete two degrees but extend the time to complete one. For example, an MBA and J.D. can be earned in four years instead of five for each separately.

Professional School

Medical School

In spite of a climate of uncertainty in health care, medical schools have received a record number of applications for three consecutive years. Although superior grades and MCAT scores are important, medical schools also screen for personal traits and related experience. Successful applicants often demonstrate an early motivation for service through volunteer work in a health or community setting: for example, they began volunteering as college freshmen or sophomores with hospital patients, battered women, or abused children.

Thirty universities select exceptionally well qualified high school seniors for programs that combine undergraduate and medical school education. Students can graduate from such a combined program in six years as compared to eight for the usual sequence of separate programs. Your child should refer to the annual *Medical School Admission Requirements*, published by the Association of American Medical Colleges, for a list of these institutions.

Pre-med students may choose any undergraduate major as long as they complete necessary prerequisites: two years of chemistry, one year each of biology and physics (with labs), and one year of calculus. (Requirements vary by medical school.) Your child should obtain a broad education in the sciences and liberal arts to be an attractive medical school candidate and to provide other options if not admitted.

Your child may have difficulty choosing a career direction and only decide by senior year (or later) to become a physician. Postbaccalaureate pre-med programs are available for graduates who lack prerequisites for medical school; however, this route often extends a person's education by two to three years.

Can you imagine your child devoting five to eleven years to postbaccalaureate medical education? How will he or she fare during a residency of 24-hour days and 80-hour work weeks? Will your child remain composed and think clearly in the face of life-or-death decisions about a patients' treatment? Medical school admissions officers look for signs of applicants' compassion, intensity, self-direction, and ability to make quick decisions under the pressure of emergency conditions. Some applicants have undertaken an honors thesis requiring intense, focused, independent effort or have performed volunteer work with a rescue squad.

Before completing applications, your son or daughter should identify the institutions that are a match with his or her credentials and interests. Some medical schools are more research-oriented, while others focus more on primary care. The most competitive schools accept only 4–5 percent of their applicants. Medical school applicants apply to an average of nine schools. Application to this number of schools can cost nearly $1,000. In addition, medical schools require personal interviews. Travel costs can mount quickly if your son or daughter applies to out-of-state schools. Once he or she is accepted, tuition costs may be as high as $29,000 a year at some top private institutions.

According to graduate school advisers, many pre-med students feel family pressure to enter medical school. Yet surveys indicate that 30–50 percent of physicians would choose a different career if they could make the decision again. An increasing number of doctors are seeking counseling for stress and burnout. Your child should conduct information interviews with physicians to determine the advantages and disadvantages of entering the medical profession.

Business School

Could your child become one of the new "super-MBAs," a "corporate triathlete" or "techno-MBA?" These terms describe students who enroll in a curriculum that blends business, engineering, and computer science. Other students may specialize in MBA programs that focus on fields such as arts, entertainment, and media management; international business; quality management; nonprofit management; or real estate development.

An MBA is a particularly good background for those who aspire to senior-level management responsibilities or to entrepreneurship. Some career fields, such as brand management, are difficult to enter without an MBA. In addition, an MBA is usually necessary to advance within some fields, such as investment banking and consulting.

The most competitive MBA programs prefer to accept applicants who have two to five years of substantive full-time work experience. Admissions officers strive to select a diverse student body. A typical entering class may include students who have been employed by large corporations, investment banks, consulting firms, nonprofits, the military, small import-export firms, and hospitals.

Some students think of business schools' requirement of (or at least strong preference for) work experience as an obstacle—they would like to enroll in an MBA program immediately following college graduation. However, MBA students who have work experience enjoy several advantages over those who do not. Experienced students are more likely to be focused about their career goals. It is easier for them to absorb the difficult course content since they have encountered similar issues and problems on the job. They are more marketable in their job search, as employers seek those with related experience. Average starting salaries are $20,000 higher for experienced MBA students compared to inexperienced ones. Experienced students also add depth to class discussions of case studies and to study groups.

Top-tier business schools accept a small percentage of outstanding applicants who do not have full-time work experience. These college students typically display a stellar record of achievement: academic honors; leadership in extracurricular, community, or volunteer activities; and internship or entrepreneurial experience. Less-selective business schools usually accept a higher proportion of inexperienced applicants.

Many MBA students at top schools (such as Harvard, Northwestern, Stanford, and MIT) have previously held jobs paying about $60,000 a year. The cost of the MBA degree could total $160,000 or more (including foregone income for two years, tuition, and other expenses). Starting compensation after obtaining the MBA may be as high as $70,000–100,000, including signing bonus (a one-time payment received upon acceptance of the job offer). For MBA graduates of lower-ranked schools, compensation may start in the twenties or thirties.

Your child does not need to major in business as an undergraduate in order to attend business school. Many schools actually prefer other majors. Since most MBA programs are heavily quantitative, your son or daughter should consider taking some undergraduate courses in areas such as calculus, accounting, statistics, operations research, and economics to prepare for graduate business education. Some schools offer pre-MBA courses in the summer for new first-year students who need to sharpen their quantitative or computer skills. Other alternatives include tutoring and additional classes while enrolled in business school.

Getting an MBA typically requires two years of full-time study. At some institutions, such as Baylor University (Waco, Texas), students with an under-graduate business degree may complete the degree in one year.

Students in a two-year MBA program often receive assistance obtaining internships during the summer after their first year. The Darden Graduate School of Business Administration at the University of Virginia offers a three-year sequence for new college graduates that includes a 15-month paid intern-ship. This program targets liberal arts and engineering majors with high-caliber academic and leadership backgrounds. Nonaccounting majors may receive a 15-month M.S. in Accounting/MBA degree at Northeastern University and obtain a paid internship with a "Big Six" accounting firm. The result is a 100 percent employment rate for graduates.

Some MBA internships are available in foreign countries. Students at "Thunderbird," The American Graduate School of International Manage-ment, have held internships with organizations such as Coca-Cola in China and Scott Paper in Hong Kong; other interns have worked in countries such as Russia, France, and Japan. Pepperdine's master of international business program allows students to intern in France or Germany to complement their courses in international business and foreign language.

Graduates of 34 participating MBA schools (including Columbia, Harvard, Indiana, and the University of North Carolina at Chapel Hill) may apply to the MBA Enterprise Corps to gain experience in international business. Those selected spend an average of 15 months in Central Europe, Asia, or Africa following graduation helping local firms make the transition from a socialist to a free-market economy.

Law School

Does your child have keen writing and analytic skills? A logical mind? The ability to think quickly and not be fazed by confrontation? Is he or she thorough and detail oriented? Law could be just the right field.

Many students, however, choose a law career without doing adequate research on the profession. It seems like the default position for undecided students. One student, Miguel, decided to attend law school after friends and family kept pointing out, "It's perfect. You love to argue!" Even students with a long-standing interest in the field sometimes find that law school is not at all what they had expected. The curriculum may seem tedious and formulaic as students learn to "think like a lawyer." Media portrayals of lawyers who work on high-profile trials, or serve as advocates for worthwhile causes or groups, are often appealing. The daily experience of most lawyers is much different, though: legal research and preparation of legal documents can be painstaking and routine.

Pre-law students should obtain a broad education. They may choose any college major. If your child aspires to become a lawyer, he or she should develop excellent writing, research, analytic, and public speaking skills through course selection, extracurricular activities, and volunteer or work experience. The debate team, student government or honor court, and mediation training are all helpful experiences. Your son or daughter should conduct information interviews with lawyers and seek summer or part-time positions that provide exposure to the legal environment.

Many law schools provide clinical education in which students gain practical experience representing clients in court cases under a lawyer's supervision or in moot courts (simulation cases). Your child should research the availability of these programs and the specialties offered by different law schools (such as intellectual property or environmental law) to determine which school is most suitable.

The acceptance rate at top schools is as low as 5–10 percent of applicants. New graduates of these schools earn the highest starting salaries ($83,000–95,500) at major New York law firms. By contrast, almost half of new lawyers earn salaries in the range of $25,000–40,000. Compensation also differs greatly according to the type of law practiced, with jobs in public interest or advocacy work and government paying far less than corporate law. Some law school graduates enter alternative careers, such as arbitrator, FBI agent, legal researcher, politician, and lobbyist.

Law can be a prestigious and lucrative career choice, with the opportunity to share in the profits as a partner in a law firm. However, large firms promote only about one in eight lawyers to partner within seven to nine years, and the others leave under an "up or out" policy. As a result, "law is one of the few fields where young professionals become less marketable as they get more experience," according to a *Wall Street Journal* article. Establishing a solo practice can be difficult, as it takes time to develop clients. A survey of lawyers in the California Bar Association revealed that 75 percent would not recommend law as a profession to their children.

Other Professional Programs (Veterinary, Dental, and Social Work)

Veterinary, dental, and social work programs are additional examples of professional schools. A young person with science ability, manual dexterity, the ability to comfort animals and establish rapport with their owners, and composure in emergency situations may want to consider a career in veterinary medicine. Job outlook for veterinarians is expected to be good as pet ownership continues to rise. Doctors of veterinary medicine (D.V.M.'s or V.M.D.'s) complete four years at a college of veterinary medicine. Some veterinarians specialize in the care of pets, such as dogs, cats, and birds. Others treat livestock, laboratory animals, wildlife, or marine animals. Veterinarians may become certified in areas such as dermatology, surgery, and dentistry after three years of additional education. Opportunities for veterinarians exist in private practice, research, food safety inspection, and education.

If your child is interested in veterinary medicine, he or she should take courses in biology, chemistry, physics, and calculus. Experience working with animals in settings such as a veterinarian's office, zoo, or animal shelter is also desirable. Since most veterinary colleges are public institutions, they tend to favor in-state residents. The average starting salary for veterinarians in private practice is $30,694; potential income for experienced veterinarians may exceed $90,000 a year.

If your child has science aptitude, manual dexterity, and good spatial perception and communication skills, he or she may want to explore dentistry as a career. Undergraduate course work for pre-dental students should include biology, chemistry, and physics. Applicants should try to obtain health-related experience such as work in a dentist's office. Dental school requires four years of study, and graduates receive the doctor of dental surgery (D.D.S.) or doctor of dental medicine (D.M.D.) degree.

Some dentists are general practitioners, and others specialize in areas such as orthodontia, pediatric dentistry, or periodontics (treatment of gum disease). Specialization requires two to four years of additional education following dental school. Although job growth for dentists is projected to be slower than average for all occupations, this will be offset by admission of fewer students to dental school than in the 1980s. There are six fewer dental schools than there were a decade ago. Dentists in private practice earn the highest incomes. Median net income for self-employed dentists is $90,000, with specialists earning as much as $130,000.

Is your child interested in helping others, and able to be compassionate and objective while dealing with others' difficult problems? Social work may be a career field to consider. A master's of social work (M.S.W.) is a marketable degree, and employment opportunities for graduates are projected to increase faster than average. Whereas a Ph.D. is required for licensure as a psychologist, the M.S.W. is a terminal degree that qualifies a social worker for many counseling positions. Social work is a broad field, including practice in medical social work, school social work, employee assistance programs, child welfare and family services, gerontological services, mental health, and corrections. Home health care and gerontological services are growth areas in social work. A social worker may establish a private practice, work as a caseworker or supervisor in a nonprofit or government agency, teach, or conduct research. Burnout is a problem for some social workers as they deal with client problems and high-volume case loads.

At some universities students with a bachelor's in social work may be able to complete an M.S.W. in less time than the two years it normally requires. Students with other majors who are interested in social work should take undergraduate course work in social sciences such as psychology, sociology, political science, and economics. Social services experience, whether paid or volunteer work, is recommended before students apply to graduate school in social work.

Graduate School

Doctoral Degrees

Is your child passionately interested in his or her major? Would you characterize your child as high in creativity, and academic and problem-solving skills? Has he or she demonstrated the ability to take initiative and be self-directed by carrying out a research project such as an honors thesis or independent study? Does your child have the perseverance and intensity to complete a lengthy period of training of four to six years or more? Is he or she interested in college teaching and research? If so, graduate school in his or her chosen field may be the right option.

The Ph.D. (doctor of philosophy) degree provides students with broad knowledge in their field (such as political science, biology, or English) and trains them to do independent research to discover new knowledge. Graduate students spend the first several years taking classes, culminating in comprehensive written or oral examinations, or both. Next, students conduct research on a topic approved by a faculty committee. If your child is interested in pursuing a Ph.D., it is helpful for him or her to think in advance about possible research interests.

Jamal called a university to inquire about an application to study for a Ph.D. in history.

The admissions representative asked, "Which area?"

Jamal responded, "American history."

There was an expectant pause. He added, "*Colonial* American history," an answer which was accepted.

Students should consult faculty members for recommendations of well-regarded graduate schools in their discipline. What are the areas of research for which each of the schools is known? Which faculty members at those institutions may be suitable mentors, based on their specialties and publications?

Many Ph.D. programs require proficiency in one or more foreign languages, such as German for psychology students and Greek and Latin for classics students. Graduate schools often prefer at least a 3.4 GPA in an applicant's major. Students with lower grades may want to enroll first in a master's degree program to prove that they are capable of graduate-level work.

Even if an applicant meets all the minimum criteria for acceptance (such as prerequisites, GPA, admissions test scores), competition is keen. In one psychology Ph.D. program, 906 students applied for 28 spaces. One study concluded that more than four out of ten Ph.D. students drop out before completion of their degree. For those who do obtain a doctorate, competition for jobs remains fierce. As many as 300 applicants vie for each job opening in fields such as the humanities. It is common for Ph.D. graduates to begin their career in one-year appointments or part-time positions.

Science Ph.D. graduates interested in academic jobs often need to work as "postdocs," apprentice scientists at a university, before obtaining a tenure-track position. Research universities employ far fewer Ph.Ds in science and engineering than in the past. Only 31 percent of science and engineering doctorate recipients in the years 1983–86 had achieved tenure or were in tenure-track posts by 1991. Mathematicians, engineers, and scientists also face competition from laid-off defense industry employees with the end of the Cold War. Employers find that applicants with Ph.Ds from the former Soviet Union and Eastern Europe are willing to work for much lower wages than Americans, further contributing to a tight job market.

Starting salaries vary widely by field for doctorate recipients, even for jobs at the same institution. An assistant professor in business may earn over $50,000, whereas a faculty member of the same rank in psychology may earn $20,000 less. Faculty members with doctorates in business, engineering, computer science, health, and physical science tend to fare better than those in fields such as liberal arts. Ph.D. graduates in all fields typically receive higher salaries outside colleges and universities.

Master's Degrees

A master's degree is less time consuming, less expensive, and less intensive than a doctorate and is sufficient preparation to qualify for many career fields. A master's in education is generally necessary for school guidance counselors or college student personnel professionals, and a master's in library or information science is desirable for those interested in becoming librarians. Archivist or curator positions require a master's degree.

A master's in social work is necessary for many social services positions. Geriatric care managers qualify for their positions with a bachelor's in nursing or gerontology and a master's in social work. Those with a master's degree in social science or public health are qualified for positions in social or behavioral research. Urban and regional planners with a master's in public administration are more competitive for government jobs than bachelor's graduates.

Applicants in several health occupations, like public health, hospital administration, and physical therapy, find these fields easier to enter with a master's degree. A master's degree is required for speech language pathologists and audiologists.

Students with a master's degree in chemistry, computer science, operations research, and statistics are marketable for many positions in industry. Pharmacoeconomics is a new career for economics or pharmacology majors who obtain a master's in economics.

A master's degree in a liberal arts field, such as English or history, is the minimum qualification to teach at a junior college. However, Ph.D. candidates also apply for these positions and are considered more qualified. A master's degree in these fields may not increase a student's marketability for positions in business or industry.

Bachelor's degree accounting programs are being phased out in favor of master's degree programs, since by the year 2000 accounting students will require five years of course work to sit for the CPA exam. This trend for institutions to convert bachelor's to master's degree programs is expected to impact other fields, such as pharmacy, already a five-year bachelor's degree at many institutions.

Tips for Graduate School Applications

The process of applying to graduate school requires approximately one year, so your child should send for applications at least two semesters before graduation. Many factors are evaluated by admissions officers: grades, the personal essay, recommendations, the graduate school admission test, work and extracurricular experience, and in some cases a personal interview.

The Personal Essay

Graduate and professional school applications typically request a personal statement or autobiographical essay. MBA program applications usually ask seven or eight deliberately ambiguous, open-ended questions. After writing and rewriting the application for days or weeks, your child may show it to you and ask, "What do you think?" An objective perspective can be helpful.

How can you critique a personal statement or essay question? Here are some factors to consider:

Is it interesting? The beginning of the statement should be strong and memorable. A storytelling style is effective—a term paper tone is not. Imagine that you are an admissions officer reading thousands of applications. Will it stand out in a positive way?

Is it persuasive? Think of the essay as a written version of an interview. Does your child make an effective case for admission? If three-fourths of the applicants are qualified, would this essay make the cut into the top 10 to 15 percent? Is it clear what motivates your child to enter business (or medical, or law) school, and why this program is the right choice?

Does it answer the question? Some applications are ten pages long, and students are tempted to recycle the same answer to more than one school even when there are subtle differences in the questions. The responses should be relevant and targeted. Your child should avoid too many references to high school accomplishments in favor of those which are more current.

Does it describe your child's distinctive qualities, skills, experience, or background? Schools strive for diversity in their student body. Your child may not realize what is unique or special about his or her qualifications. Perhaps you will be able to point out relevant information that was left out or that should be emphasized. What will he or she add to the program?

Is it well written and error free? The essay is a writing sample. In addition to content, it is judged on grammar, punctuation, and spelling.

Does it sound genuine and sincere? Your child should not try to anticipate what the admissions committee wants to hear. There is not one perfect answer to an essay question.

Recommendations

You may be tempted to suggest a prominent family friend as a reference. For example, law schools receive many recommendations from judges and members of Congress. Unless this person knows your child well and has strong ties to the school, someone else may be able to write a more effective recommendation.

Faculty members, previous or current supervisors, and administrators who have observed your child in leadership roles are usually the most helpful references. Has your daughter assisted a faculty member with a laboratory research project? This professor's remarks would be valuable for her application for graduate study in chemistry. If your son is a star on the debate team, the club's adviser could attest to his analytic and persuasive skills for law school admission.

Your child should ask whether a prospective reference feels comfortable providing a recommendation. "I'm planning to apply to graduate school in political science. Do you feel you know my work well enough to give me a good recommendation?"

After identifying several references, your child should set up an appointment with each one to discuss his or her career goals and plans for further study. He or she should give them a draft of the application, résumé, and transcript. Recommenders may be able to effectively critique an essay or personal statement. They may remind a student to mention an overlooked project, or suggest information to de-emphasize.

Many college career offices provide a reference service for graduate school applications. Recommenders complete one form, which is copied and mailed by the career office to all the universities to which your child applies. These may be confidential (your child waives the right to read them) or not. Confidential forms usually carry more weight with admissions officers; some faculty members decline to complete a form that is not confidential.

If the reference forms are not going to be sent by the career office, your child should give each recommender a form with a stamped, addressed envelope and specify application deadlines. Some recommenders will need a gentle reminder to ensure that all supporting materials are received in time. Many schools indicate that they have a "rolling admissions" policy, making decisions on applications as they receive them. Your son or daughter's early application is an advantage in this process.

....

"So, where are you going to graduate school?" a classmate asked Michael.

"I am wait-listed at several schools. They wrote that I would have been accepted if my application had been received sooner. Several of my recommendations arrived late. I must not have been clear enough about when I needed the forms mailed, and I didn't follow up on them. It's still possible that another student will decide to go elsewhere and I'll get in."

....

It is appropriate for your son or daughter to send a typed thank-you letter to recommenders, expressing appreciation for their time. Your child should also follow up with them to share good news about acceptance to graduate school and about his or her decision where to enroll.

Is your child planning to take time off before applying to graduate school? It is often more difficult to obtain faculty references after graduation, as professors may retire or change jobs. Also, faculty may not remember your child as clearly with the passage of time. The ideal time to request letters of reference is early in the fall semester of senior year for students not taking time off, and before graduation for those who plan to delay application to graduate school. Some faculty prefer students to request a reference after completion of their course.

Graduate School Admission Exams

By junior year your child needs to determine the required admissions tests (see Table 6.2) for the graduate or professional programs in which he or she is interested, and the timing needed to ensure that the results arrive before admission deadlines.

It is important for your son or daughter to prepare for a graduate or professional school admissions exam. Many colleges and universities offer free assistance with test-taking skills. Your child may also purchase books and computer software to become familiar with test format and general content. Commercial firms such as Princeton Review and Stanley Kaplan offer in-depth test preparation through classroom instruction, practice tests, and home study materials. Adam took a free diagnostic test from a test preparation service and scored in the 63rd percentile on the GMAT. Following his enrollment in their GMAT course, he scored in the 89th percentile on the test. Many parents believe that a commercial test preparation service is worth the investment (up to $825) to help their children compete for highly selective graduate programs.

If your child plans to delay graduate school admission for a year or more after college, he or she should take the required admissions exam before graduation. According to the Graduate Management Admission Council (GMAC), test scores tend to be higher for those who are still in college. A GMAC representative suggests that students take admissions tests while in college and "bank the score," as the scores are usually accepted for three to five years after they are earned.

Your child should not plan to take a test "cold," with the intention of retaking it. Although students may generally take an admissions exam more than once, their three most recent scores in the last five years are reported to the graduate schools to which they apply. Test takers may hope to score higher on a second test and actually perform worse. A graduate school may consider the highest score, the most recent score, or the average of the two. Most students do study for these exams—some prepare for as much as six months through a test preparation service.

Grades

Whereas some programs are so competitive that a stratospheric GPA is a must, other graduate schools are more interested in grades achieved in upper-level (junior and senior year) classes or in an applicant's major. It can be a disadvantage for a transcript to reflect many courses taken pass/fail. Admissions officers also consider the level of difficulty of the courses and the reputation of the institution at which they were taken.

Interviews

Many graduate or professional schools require an interview as part of the application process. Your child may be expected to visit universities where he or she has applied. In other cases an admissions officer may conduct a telephone interview or ask a graduate who lives near your son or daughter to schedule an interview. The meeting may take place before a student's completed application is received, so an applicant should respond to questions as if the interviewer has not read about his or her background.

Adding Up the Costs

It can be expensive to apply to graduate or professional school. Here are examples of costs:

Admissions Test Preparation and Registration

Test preparation—Although the testing service publisher may offer a free booklet about the exam, most registrants also use additional materials such as books ($15–40), computer software ($50–60), and commercial test preparation services (up to $825). A test preparation service may discount course tuition 40 percent for students who can document that they are receiving financial aid.

Admissions tests—Costs range from $35 (PCAT) to $155 (MCAT). Students with financial hardship may apply for a fee waiver for some tests.

Centralized application processing services—Most law schools require applicants to subscribe to the Law School Data Assembly Service, which sends transcripts, writing samples, and an academic summary to law schools specified by an applicant. Many medical schools require applicants to use the American Medical College Application Service. These services cost approximately $100–250 for students who apply to the average number of law or medical schools. In addition, each school typically requires a supplementary application with a separate fee.

Application Fees and Other Costs

Application fees—Depending on the graduate or professional school, these fees range from about $35 to $75 each. If your child applies to 10 or 11 schools, the costs add up quickly.

Personal interviews—Some programs, such as medical schools, require personal interviews as part of the application process. Travel expenses can mount when your son or daughter applies to out-of-state schools.

Transcripts and reference services—Students are usually charged for each transcript. Most universities offer a reference service (for a fee) to assemble a packet of references, a résumé, and other application materials, which are mailed to specified schools.

Deposits

Once your child has been accepted, most schools require a nonrefundable deposit to hold his or her place. This deposit might be needed to meet the school's deadline while your child is hoping for acceptance by a more desirable graduate school. A deposit could cost about $200.

Timing of Graduate Study

Even if your child is accepted into graduate or professional school, his or her plans may change for other reasons. Many students suddenly decide during spring of their senior year to take time off from education before making a commitment to a demanding course of study. Other circumstances may alter or delay your child's graduate school plans, such as changes in family financial circumstances. A backup plan is valuable in these situations.

Deferred enrollment is an option sometimes available to students. Graduate schools are often supportive of delayed matriculation, since they value students with additional maturity and certainty about their goals. Students may, however, need to reapply for financial aid when they are ready to enroll.

Many students say that they believe that graduate study is a now-or-never proposition. Once they become accustomed to a job with a steady income, they reason, it will be much more difficult to return to college. For some students that may be true.

However, there can be good reasons to delay graduate education. Not every college senior is certain about a career direction. Work experience may help a graduate clarify strengths, weaknesses, and interests. It may help in determining whether further education is necessary. Graduate school applicants often have more maturity and stronger qualifications as a result of working several years.

Some organizations offer generous tuition reimbursement plans for employees who take job-related courses part-time, which helps avoid heavy debt. Other employers may fund the entire cost of graduate study, sometimes allowing the employee to attend full-time with the stipulation that he or she will return to work for a specified length of time after graduation. For example, the military covers the cost of medical or law school for very competitive applicants, who incur a military obligation upon graduation.

Some financial analysts at investment banks, described as "rare stars" by one employer, may be reimbursed their MBA school tuitions if they return after graduation. They commit to remain with the firm for at least three or four years.

The Big Six accounting firms in some metropolitan areas recruit at selected colleges (such as Harvard, Wellesley, Princeton, Colgate, and Babson) that do not offer an accounting curriculum. These graduates join public accounting offices in New York City, Boston, Chicago, or San Francisco at 70–80 percent of the salary offered to accounting majors. In addition to salary and benefits, the liberal arts hires receive 15 months' release time from work to attend accounting classes full- or part-time during their first 18 months with the firm.

What If Your Child Isn't Accepted?

Despite an intense desire to become a lawyer (veterinarian, dentist, psychologist, etc.) and impressive credentials, your son or daughter may not be accepted into graduate or professional school. Many students are ill-prepared to begin a job search when they receive rejection letters from graduate schools as late as April or May of their senior year. Attractive employers have often filled their openings through on-campus interviewing by February or March.

Encourage your child to prepare a backup plan as an alternative to graduate or professional school. What are some ways to do this? Even though your son is applying to law school, he could also interview for positions as a policy analyst, legal assistant, probation officer, or campaign worker for a political candidate. If your daughter is applying to medical school, she could also interview for openings as a pharmaceutical sales representative, staff consultant for a firm specializing in the health care industry, or research technician at a hospital. As one medical school admissions officer put it, "People with backup plans are probably less likely to need them—they have prepared themselves with a broad perspective instead of doggedly pursuing one narrow goal." Students applying to extremely competitive programs, such as clinical psychology, may want to apply to related professional school programs, such as counseling or educational psychology.

Students are often eternal optimists when it comes to their graduate school prospects. "I'll reapply next year," your son may reassure you following rejection by all five or ten schools to which he applied. Graduate school admissions officers say that students may obtain useful feedback by asking why they were turned down. Would it help next time around if your son took additional upper-level courses in his major? Perhaps related work experience would tip the scales in his favor. However, if nothing changes in the intervening year or so between applications, the result is likely to be the same.

Some applicants are accepted to graduate school after reapplying. It reflects positively on their maturity if they have used the intervening time productively. A medical school admissions officer, asked for examples of worthwhile activities during a year between applications, retorted, "Not lounging in Cancun or Ft. Lauderdale!" One student volunteered with Mother Theresa for a year in India and found medical school admissions officers eager to interview her. Other examples of constructive experience include the Peace Corps, Teach for America, laboratory research work, and educational outreach programs for public health departments.

Applicants should show a willingness to move on with their lives instead of waiting indefinitely for acceptance; they should write a new essay when they reapply to reflect their activities and growth since their original application.

If placed on a waiting list, your son or daughter should follow up periodically with the admissions office. A wait-list student could be notified of acceptance as late as the day before classes begin if someone else drops out suddenly.

Special Programs

Some college graduates enroll in short-term educational programs designed to provide specific career-related skills. Examples are paralegal training, business and publishing institutes, and a design program.

Paralegal School

The paralegal field is the fastest-growing occupation, according to the U.S. Department of Labor. Paralegals may conduct interviews with clients and witnesses, research records such as titles and deeds, draft wills and trusts, and perform many other duties to assist lawyers.

Although students at some universities may obtain a bachelor's degree in paralegal studies, graduates with other majors can also acquire these skills through three- to six-month programs at paralegal schools. The schools typically provide employment assistance for their graduates. Students may choose a school that offers generalist training or one with the option to specialize in areas such as litigation, employee benefits, or real estate. According to Andrea Wagner, author of *How to Land Your First Paralegal Job*, senior paralegals in specialty areas may earn as much as $60,000–80,000 a year. Some paralegal schools are ABA-approved.

Formal paralegal education is not always necessary, as some employers hire new college graduates and provide them with on-the-job training for these positions. For graduates who take time off before law school, a paralegal or legal assistant position may be an ideal temporary, transitional job. They have an opportunity to observe the legal profession in practice and can more realistically decide whether to attend law school.

Publishing Institutes

Did your child enjoy working on a high school or college publication or in a book store or library? Does he or she have strong skills in writing, photography, graphic arts, marketing, or public relations? Such a student may benefit from attending a publishing institute to explore this career field, develop further related skills, and network with book and magazine publishing professionals.

The Radcliffe Publishing Course in Cambridge, Massachusetts, offers six weeks of "total immersion." This demanding course requires students, who must be college graduates, to complete ten advance assignments before they arrive. The program costs $4,435, including room and board.

The Carolina Publishing Institute, sponsored by the University of North Carolina at Chapel Hill, allows applicants to choose up to three one-week sessions on book publishing: "Editorial," "Design and Production," and "Marketing." The program costs from $450 to $900, depending on the number of sessions, excluding housing. Rice University, the University of Denver, the University of Chicago, and New York University are other schools that offer publishing programs.

Business Institutes

Nonbusiness majors may want to consider a special summer institute to acquire basic business skills before beginning their job search. The University of Virginia and Columbia University, for example, offer intensive six- and twelve-week programs, respectively, which include courses in accounting, finance, business statistics, management, and marketing. They also provide seminars for students on computer and job search skills. While the Virginia program is limited to college graduates, Columbia permits current college students to enroll. Tuition (excluding housing) for the six-week Virginia course costs $1,800; the twelve-week Columbia course costs $6,975. Attendance before a student's senior year is advantageous so that he or she may list the courses on a résumé and discuss them during interviews. Other universities offer similar opportunities for students to gain business skills.

Introduction to Design Careers

Harvard University offers a six-week summer program, "Career Discovery," to introduce high school students, college students, and college graduates to careers in architecture, landscape architecture, and urban design. Participants gain exposure to the design field and are able to evaluate whether they have the interest and potential to pursue a related degree. This intense program includes lectures, studio work, career counseling, and field trips. It is sponsored by the Harvard University Graduate School of Design and costs $1850; housing costs an additional $715.

One-Year Graduate Programs

Graduates of any major can obtain professional credentials in a one-year master's degree program in fields such as accounting or school counseling. These programs typically last a full 12 months.

The Massachusetts Institute of Technology offers a one-year master's in engineering, targeted at engineering bachelor's degree recipients who are interested in application-oriented course work rather than research. Graduates with a bachelor's in education and an A-level teaching certificate may earn a master's in special education or early childhood education at some institutions in one year.

Certification Programs

Noneducation majors may qualify for a teaching certificate by taking two or three terms of course work. Even without this background students in majors such as mathematics, physical sciences, and foreign languages are often hired because of critical shortage of certified teachers in these areas. Some states require noneducation majors to pursue teacher certification through "lateral entry" programs. They enroll in education courses during evenings or summers.

College graduates may prepare for other employment options through enrollment in certificate programs for teaching English as a second language, computer programming, or real estate appraisal. Health careers may be entered with one-year postbaccalaureate certificates in fields such as medical records administration or cytotechnology.

Summary

Reasons to Attend Graduate or Professional School

- An advanced degree may be required to enter a desired career field.

- An advanced degree will make a job applicant more marketable and will likely result in higher compensation (for some career fields)

- Sheer joy of learning

Reasons Not to Attend Graduate School

- Lack of a career focus

- Pressure from friends or family

- Misconceptions about the job market
- Lack of maturity
- Unrealistic expectations about graduate school

What to Do When Considering Graduate School

- Determine career goals first
- Meet with graduate and professional school advisers
- Research course prerequisites, optimum timing for admissions tests, helpful extracurricular activities, and other preparation for graduate/professional study
- Have a backup plan

Typical Graduate School Admission Applications Components

- **Personal essay statement** that has been written in an interesting, narrative style
- **Recommendations** (meet with recommenders beforehand if possible)
- **Graduate admissions test** (test preparation is necessary)
- **Transcript** (grades are important with grades in major and upper-level courses generally being weighted more heavily)

Conversation Starters for Parents and Students

1. Why do you want to go to graduate/professional school?
2. What kind of qualifications do you need to be competitive for graduate study?
3. Which faculty members or advisers do you think would be good references? What do you think each would say about you?

4. Have you considered doing a research or independent study project?

5. What preparation do you think you will need to do your best on the admissions test?

6. Do you want to take time off before graduate school? What would you do?

7. Have you considered a backup plan to graduate school?

8. How many schools do you plan to apply to? What expenses do you expect during the application process? Have you thought about how to finance graduate study?

CHAPTER 7

TAKING TIME OFF AFTER COLLEGE

Brent told his friends that he had a plan following graduation. He would hold a map, close his eyes, and go for a year to the city where his finger landed. The result? A year in Santa Fe.

You are probably thinking (or hoping) that surely your child won't be so impetuous. Many students, however, decide to take a year or more off after college graduation. Some may feel burnt out after four or five years of college and want a break before entering graduate school. Others say, "I don't want a 'real job' yet." What *do* they want? "Oh, something fun and different—not an eight-to-five desk job," as one student explained.

Students have many reasons for wanting to take time off after graduation (see checklist below). If your child is considering doing so, it may be helpful to ask about his or her motivation to help him or her identify the types of experiences that will be most satisfying.

Here are some examples of time-off pursuits that appeal to many new graduates.

Travel, study, or work abroad

- Teaching English in a foreign country

- Volunteer work

- Internships or paid work abroad

REASONS FOR TAKING TIME OFF

Students: Check the statements that characterize your reasons for wanting to take time off:

❏   1. I'm not sure what I want to do and need time to explore possibilities and make some decisions.

❏   2. I feel burned out and don't have the energy to begin a demanding career or graduate degree.

❏   3. I want to work, travel, and/or study abroad to enhance my foreign language skills or experience a different culture.

❏   4. I want to study further, or volunteer or work at a short-term position to develop additional skills and confidence before conducting a job search.

❏   5. I want to work in a fun job (dude ranch, cruise ship, resort, etc.) before settling down to a more traditional, career-oriented position.

❏   6. I want to be geographically close to someone special for a period of time before making a commitment to a career or graduate school, which may require a separation.

❏   7. I want to make a meaningful contribution through public service, religious, or volunteer work.

❏   8. I want to test out a possible career field before making a commitment (e.g., work as a legal assistant before entering law school).

❏   9. I want to do something adventurous that I may not have another opportunity to experience (Outward Bound, travel to a foreign country, etc.).

❏   10. I want to gain broad exposure to many industries, career fields, and prospective employers.

Check responses with Answer Key on page 147

- International study programs
- Independent travel

Domestic volunteer work or internship

- Working for a nonprofit agency
- Volunteering for a religious organization
- Working for a political campaign, member of Congress, or lobbying or social activist group

Temporary or contract work

- Working for a variety of industries, companies, and departments

Adventure or hospitality industry jobs

- Working for a dude ranch, resort, theme park, tour escort, or cruise ship

Nondegree study programs (see Chapter 6)

- Postbaccalaureate programs such as a business institute or publishing institute

Two-year analyst or other short-term positions

- Working as an analyst for an investment bank, real estate, or consulting firm
- Working as a legal assistant for a law firm or district attorney's office

Parents may be skeptical about the value of options that delay their child's job search or graduate school enrollment. You may wonder how this experience will be evaluated by prospective employers or admissions officers and question whether your child's interest in time off is a sign of an inability to make a commitment or accept responsibility.

Advantages and Disadvantages

Advantages

There are several advantages to taking time off: Your child could become more certain about a career direction through temporary, volunteer, or other short-term work. With additional perspective, maturity, and experience, your child may avoid a poor fit in that first "real" job.

An interim period may give a graduate who truly is burned out a chance to "recharge batteries" so he or she is able to approach a real job or graduate school with energy and commitment. Some alumni express regrets about **not** having taken the opportunity to travel or perform extended volunteer work before they assumed financial, job, or family commitments.

For future careers with a global focus, such as international business or international development, there is no substitute for living and working abroad for enhancing cross-cultural and language skills. Postgraduation may be an optimal time to obtain this experience before other commitments make it more difficult. Some graduates develop or enhance skills and obtain valuable experiences that increase their marketability for future employment or credentials for graduate school admission. For many nonprofit jobs and professional school admissions, volunteer work is especially beneficial. Students may also earn educational benefits from some volunteer organizations that will assist with the cost of future graduate study.

Disadvantages

Although your child may feel he or she has valid reasons to take time off, some employers evaluate this negatively. What are some employer assumptions that your child may encounter following a return from time off?

This applicant:

- does not have a strong work ethic and is not eager to begin a real job.

- lacks maturity and places more importance on travel, leisure time, or "self-discovery" than on employment, or is content to live off of his or her parents indefinitely.

- lacks job-related skills. (Employers may not recognize marketable skills in nontraditional settings such as dude ranches. A graduate may have to be persuasive to convey the valuable elements of hospitality jobs, such as public contact, customer service, and teamwork.)

- has been unable to find a job. Perhaps this person does not interview well, has poor references, or has other drawbacks. (Gaps in employment are often assumed to be involuntary.)

Major employers often structure management training programs to coincide with college graduation schedules. Training programs generally begin in June or August, with job offers extended to applicants as early as the preceding January. Some new graduates take several months off to travel and return home ready to start a job search. The result can be many missed opportunities. (Some employers allow students to defer their starting date of employment. One New York bank offers students their choice of starting dates in June, August, or October. The October training class fills up first, giving new hires a chance to travel or otherwise take time off.)

Employers consider it legitimate to ask why an applicant has delayed the job search. So your son or daughter should be prepared to answer the question, "What have you been doing since graduation?" Spending all summer at the beach sounds far less impressive than working for a temporary service while preparing to relocate with a spouse.

When asked about time-off experiences, one recruiter noted that "grades and college activities fade in importance with time." What is an employer's first impression of John's résumé during his senior year at college? He is an honors student and senior class president. One or two years later, he is identified just as quickly by his occupation: a waiter at a resort.

Some graduates find that a job in a glamorous location is hard to leave after a summer or a year. Consider it from their perspective: They enjoy an environment with beaches, mountains, or a desert and a ready social life with other recent graduates. The prospect of searching for a real job seems distinctly unappealing.

Each time-off experience should be considered on its own merits. This chapter provides an overview of possible options for students interested in this type of experience.

International Options

Many students want to acquire or enhance foreign language skills, particularly if they aspire to jobs in international business, foreign affairs, or other work requiring fluency in a foreign language. They may also want to travel, experience a different culture, or volunteer to help make a difference in a developing country. Some possibilities for obtaining international experience are teaching English in a foreign country, study-abroad programs, internships, volunteer work, language study programs, and independent travel. An Internet Web site providing tips about working and living overseas may be found at http://www.magi.com/˜issi/.

Evaluating International Experiences

Your daughter wants to go to Japan to teach English—or to a Yugoslavian work camp to restore historical monuments—or to wait tables in London. Her excitement is almost contagious. "This is the chance of a lifetime," she says, "I will get to travel and gain international experience, and it will help me get a job later." But you have concerns. Not too long ago you worried how she would adjust to life 200 miles away at State University. Now she wants to go thousands of miles away!

Each day you think of another concern: Will she be safe? What if she has a medical emergency? Where will she live? How much will it *really* cost? Will this experience be just a pleasant detour, unrelated to her future goals and throwing her off track?

Here are some questions to ask your daughter about travel abroad, particularly if she will be affiliated with a structured program, such as the Japanese Exchange and Teaching (JET) Program or work camps.

Organization sponsorship—What do you know about the sponsoring organization and its source of funding? Is it affiliated with another agency? If so, which one? Are its goals consistent with your values?

Health and safety—Will the program provide health insurance? If so, what does it cover? Is local health care adequate? Which immunizations do you need before leaving the United States?

Training and orientation—What kind of training or orientation is provided for program participants? (It may be critical to learn about local laws or customs. For example, some countries' laws have *severe* penalties for drug use or public consumption of alcohol.)

Housing—Where will you live? How difficult is it to obtain housing? Are there other options, such as homestays (renting a room from a local family) or university dormitories?

Living and working conditions—How does the environment differ from what you are used to? If it is described as "spartan," exactly what does that mean? Will you be isolated or part of a group? Will you be the only American in the group? If the entire group is American, will the experience provide you the exposure you want to other cultures? Will the program include other participants your age?

Costs and income—What are transportation and other expenses (e.g., application fee, room and board, insurance, and tuition) for the program? Are you eligible for a salary, stipend, or deferment or cancellation of student loans during this period? Is financial assistance available?

Foreign language skills—If you are planning to live in a foreign country, are your language skills adequate? Will you receive sufficient language training through the program?

Marketability and relationship to career goals—Have you checked into how prospective employers or graduate schools evaluate this type of experience? Is there another program that would open more opportunities?

Visa status—What type of visa do you need, and how difficult is it to obtain? (Some graduates plan to work on a tourist visa, although it is illegal to do so.) What is the duration of the visa or work permit you will be issued?

Support services—How much support will the program provide if you have problems? For example, what if the housing or internship is not what you were promised, or political instability or illness make it necessary for you to leave earlier than planned? (Some organizations promise job leads that turn out to be little more than classified ads.)

Developing Countries: A Special Note

Living abroad may sound romantic to your child, but the reality may be jarring for those who go to developing countries in Eastern Europe, Southeast Asia, and Latin America. Is your child really prepared to live without electricity, hot water, heat, and air conditioning? What are the health risks? Your child should contact the Centers for Disease Control before traveling to foreign countries to determine which immunizations are advised—even if none are required.

Teaching English Abroad

Is your child qualified to teach English abroad? Surprisingly, some positions require neither previous teaching experience nor foreign language skills; however, returning teachers strongly recommend that applicants first obtain teaching or tutoring experience to qualify for more desirable assignments and to enhance their effectiveness on the job.

What kind of background have previous graduates found helpful? Some of them have served as a teaching assistant for a professor or tutor for other students. Others have volunteered as an English conversation partner for international students, taught English as a second language to immigrants, or tutored adults through a literacy program. Your son or daughter may want to enroll in a two- to four-week course for teaching English as a foreign language.

College graduates teach high school-age students in developing countries through World Teach, a program affiliated with Harvard University but open to all applicants. Participants teach for one to two years in China, Costa Rica, Africa, Poland, or Thailand. The cost to students is approximately $3,000–4,500, including travel, training, housing, and health insurance.

The Japanese Exchange and Teaching Program matches students with jobs in Japan before they leave the United States. The program, coordinated through the Japanese embassy in Washington, D.C., guarantees a generous salary, and sponsoring employers pay for round-trip airfare. Students must make a one-year commitment, which is renewable.

Other organizations that place teachers abroad include Volunteers in Asia (based at Stanford University), Princeton in Asia, the Peace Corps, and numerous other religious and nonprofit organizations. Your child's career office should be able to provide contact information for these programs.

Your child should thoroughly research a potential teaching assignment. One graduate applied to teach English in China and accepted an assignment without consulting a map. The result? He arrived in Harbin, China, and was shocked to find himself on the edge of Siberia.

Is your child self-reliant, enthusiastic, flexible, and creative? Teaching English in a foreign country is a sink-or-swim endeavor. As one former teacher put it, "Don't expect any hand-holding!"

Demand for English teachers, working conditions, and salaries vary widely among countries. Recent graduates may travel to Japan without a job and find plentiful opportunities and lucrative salaries. Similar positions are more difficult to find and salaries are generally low in China, Eastern Europe, and Africa. Working and living conditions may differ quite a bit even within the same country.

What jobs do former teachers take after finishing their commitment? Those in Japan sometimes remain in the country to apply for other opportunities as translators, writers, or editors. International banks are sometimes interested in college graduates with international experience and foreign language skills for positions working with global or emerging markets.

Some former teachers look for work in nonprofits or government agencies. One is now a recruiter for the Peace Corps after serving with that organization in South America. Another former English teacher works at the State Department for the United States Agency for International Development, which administers foreign aid; she is a contractor for the Europe and New Independent States Bureau on urban development and housing projects. The only technical program assistant without a master's degree, she is confident that her experience in Slovakia made the difference.

International Volunteer Work

Work Camps

Eric participated in a work camp in Lefkada, Greece, during the summer after his junior year in college. He worked on a project building roads with other volunteers, ages 19–35. Reflecting on the experience, Eric remarked that "it was hard physical labor—I can identify with prisoners on chain gangs!"

Work camp opportunities are described by The Council on International Educational Exchange in its annual *International Directory of Volunteer Projects*, available each April. Volunteers pay $195 and transportation costs to spend two to four weeks in a cooperative working on community projects in countries such as Lithuania, Belgium, and Morocco. Costs may be higher for some locations—as much as $2,200, including transportation, for Ghana. Most projects occur in the summer and involve work such as environmental protection, historic preservation, and construction.

Peace Corps

The Peace Corps sends over 6,000 volunteers to serve two-year assignments in approximately 90 countries in central Europe, Africa, Asia, and Latin America. Increasingly the organization seeks applicants with technical skills and work experience; the average age for volunteers is 32. New college graduates with the specialized backgrounds listed below are more competitive candidates:

- Science (especially agriculture, forestry, biology, botany, engineering, environmental science, and geology)

- Education (vocational education, special education, English as a second language, math or science, business, and social studies)

- Health (nursing, occupational or physical therapy, nutrition, and public health)

- Business (accounting, business, and management information systems)

- Planning (urban or regional planning)

Your child should consult the agency's recruiting brochures to identify "eligibility enhancements" that will help in becoming a more qualified applicant. Some skills and backgrounds that the Peace Corps seeks are foreign language skills, tutoring or teaching experience, and environmental or social services experience.

The Peace Corps provides outstanding support services for volunteers. They receive three months of training, paid expenses, a living allowance, medical and dental coverage, and deferral of certain educational loans. In the event of political instability, they are evacuated to safety.

The intensive training program includes three components: language, cross-cultural, and technical skills. One volunteer described the technical training for an adult literacy assignment as "a crash course master's degree in education." It combined lectures about teaching theory and methodology with practicum teaching experience.

Following 27 months of training and service, volunteers receive additional benefits, including a $5,400 "readjustment allowance," possible reduction of educational loans, career counseling, and noncompetitive eligibility (preferential consideration) for federal jobs.

Many employers and universities value Peace Corps experience. Some graduate schools give volunteers credit toward a master's degree. Over 50 colleges and universities offer scholarships and assistantships to returning Peace Corps volunteers.

Religious Organizations

Students and graduates of any faith are eligible for certain volunteer programs in Israel, including work on a kibbutz and archaeological digs. Many religious organizations sponsor opportunities for college students and new graduates to serve in overseas missions. They may help build a new church, school, or playground, give religious instruction to children, or teach English as a foreign language.

Internships or Work Abroad

Internships in Europe

Your child may want to combine international travel, study, and work. Internships in Europe is a program that allows students and recent graduates to integrate all three goals. This organization coordinates programs for over 100 universities in six locations: London, Brussels, Bonn/Cologne, Paris, and Madrid. The program is competitive. Students need a minimum GPA of 3.0 and should carefully prepare the application and essay. Students work at an unpaid internship for three to four days a week, attend class one day a week, and receive academic credit for the experience.

Work Abroad

The Council on International Educational Exchange (CIEE) is a nonprofit educational organization that helps college students obtain a work permit in a foreign country (Britain, Ireland, France, Germany, Canada, Costa Rica, New Zealand, or Jamaica). For a $200 fee students or recent graduates receive an orientation, job leads, and housing assistance after they arrive. (Graduates are eligible to participate for the semester following their last full-time enrollment in college.) Housing options include college dormitories, homestays with local families, and apartments. The duration of the work authorization is three to six months, depending on the country.

Trent flew to London, found a job as a waiter in a pub within three days, and spent the summer working and traveling through Europe. What did he learn? "I gained a lot of self-confidence. I was totally on my own and proved my flexibility and resourcefulness." Kate stayed less than a week. "I can get a waitress or sales clerk job at home. What was the point of staying and working at a low-paying job?"

Most of the students or graduates in the CIEE program work in restaurants, resorts, bars, and retail stores at unskilled service jobs. One London restaurant advertises for American staff:

Want to further your career in entertaining, media and broadcasting as a dancing, gum-chewing DJ at London's authentic '50s American diner—then Rock Island Diner wants you! We also need extroverted, all-dancing, all-action servers and bussers. So grease your hair back, slip on your sneakers and rock around the clock in the heart of London. Interested? Got a demo tape, photo and résumé?

Some students and recent graduates obtain paid internships or career-related jobs through CIEE.

If your child chooses this option to work abroad, he or she will probably be able to cover day-to-day expenses with earnings. However, initial costs include transportation and enough funds (approximately $600 to $1000) to get by until receipt of that first paycheck.

International Study

Language Schools

A graduate who wants to study a foreign language while immersed in another culture may consider attending a language school abroad. Courses typically last a minimum of one month, although some vary in length from two weeks to a semester or a year. Universities and private language schools offer language study programs.

Your son or daughter should evaluate factors such as location, class size, student–teacher ratio, length, cost, methods of instruction, and hours of instruction. Student–teacher ratios can be as low as four to one. Some language schools use multiple teaching methods, including conversation groups, language tapes, tutors, and field trips. Daily instruction may last four to eight hours, with additional preparation time expected out of the classroom.

Schools also may offer homestays and access to nonlanguage courses, such as art, architecture, history, and geography.

Language proficiency requirements for applicants differ by school. Some accept students without any foreign language skills; others require prospective students to pass a proficiency test or provide a transcript showing four semesters of college-level language.

Some examples of language schools include Eurocentres (France, Italy, Spain, Germany), the CET-Wellesley College Chinese Language Study Program, the British Institute of Florence, Keio University (Japan), and The Center for Bilingual Multicultural Studies (Mexico).

Specialized Study Programs

There is a study program for virtually every subject. If your child is interested in learning about art history, Sotheby's Education Studies features lectures and tours of museums and the auction house from Sotheby's experts. Three- and twelve-month programs are available.

If your child wants to explore his or her Jewish heritage, the American Zionist Youth Foundation offers a four-week program, "Graduate to Israel." This educational and social program includes tours of historic and modern areas in Israel.

Independent Travel

Many resources are available for students to review before planning travel abroad. For example, *Work, Study, Travel Abroad: The Whole World Handbook* includes profiles and advice about countries from Argentina to Zimbabwe.

Students may obtain an International Student Identity Card, which entitles them to discounts on transportation, lodging, and admission to tourist and cultural attractions. Cardholders also receive basic accidental and health insurance, and access to a toll-free hot line in case of legal, medical, and financial emergencies. The card is valid from September 1 through December 31 of the following year: spring or summer graduates may use it until the expiration date.

Domestic Volunteer Work or Internships

New graduates sometimes volunteer or accept modest wages for environmental, social activist, or nonprofit groups for a year or two. Examples of these programs follow.

Green Corps is a popular environmental lobbying group that recruits graduates interested in environmental issues. They learn to use lobbying techniques to increase citizen and legislator awareness of environmental problems. If participants work with Green Corps for 13 months, they receive a salary of $14,500 a year plus benefits.

Habitat for Humanity is a nondenominational Christian organization dedicated to building housing for low-income families. Prospective homeowners contribute "sweat equity" and buy their house with no-interest loans. Volunteers may serve for ten weeks to a year or more in the United States; they may serve overseas for a three-year commitment. Typical duties include construction, child care, fund-raising, and administration.

Camphill Village is a community for mentally or physically challenged "villagers." Volunteer coworkers work side by side with the villagers in crafts, farming, gardening, or retail jobs (such as in a gift shop or bakery). New graduates typically stay for one or two years, receiving free room and board. Camphill Villages are located in the United States and 15 other countries.

Teach for America recruits new college graduates to teach in inner-city and rural schools for two years. Designed for noneducation majors, the program sends new teachers to an intensive six-week training program before they report to their assignments. They also receive support from a mentor teacher. Up to 60 percent of the recruits have remained in teaching after completion of their obligation.

Jesuit Volunteer Corps or Lutheran Volunteer Corps are examples of organizations pursuing social justice for the needy. Participants work with the homeless, the elderly, or battered women in the inner city. Volunteers serve for a year or more as teachers, health workers, and community organizers. Room and board, insurance, and a small stipend are provided for volunteers.

New graduates may be interested in volunteering or working at entry-level jobs for members of Congress, political parties, and lobbying or advocacy groups. Especially during a campaign year, many opportunities are available to assist political candidates at the federal, state, and local levels. Recent graduates help recruit volunteers, staff telephone banks, and assist with fund-raising.

Temporary or Contract Work

Is your child flexible, personable, resourceful, and a team player? For a graduate unsure about a career direction but eager to try out a number of possibilities, temporary work may be beneficial. Where else can your child work for a publisher, university, accounting firm, and manufacturer within the same month?

Many employers are reluctant to take a risk on job applicants. Temporary and contract firms are a boon for employers who want to save recruiting, screening, and benefits costs while staffing short-term assignments.

There are a number of benefits to temporary work for college students or new graduates.

- Exposure to different industries, companies, and departments

- Potential to learn new skills on the job (including free training from temporary firms in skills that are in short supply)

- The opportunity to be considered for regular employment ("temp-to-perm" jobs)

- Additional experience to include on a résumé

- Contacts that may be useful for networking, job leads, and references

- Income during a job search, while becoming established in the arts (such as acting, painting, writing, or music), or supporting travel

Several tips will help your child make the most of temporary work. The first dilemma may be how to decide which temporary firm to contact. A graduate who wants to work for specific companies should call their human resources departments to ask which temporary firms they use. Some large employers operate an internal temporary service. If your child is interested in a certain industry or functional area, he or she should identify the agencies that specialize in these areas. It is acceptable to register with several different agencies.

Your child can have a better chance of obtaining temporary assignments by being easy to reach and flexible about availability for work. An answering machine is invaluable for a job hunter. When your child applies to temporary firms, he or she should ask about assignments more likely to lead to permanent employment (temp-to-perm) or to develop marketable skills.

Whether the job is challenging or mundane, a temporary employee—like any other employee—should try to exceed the employer's expectations. Good work performance, a positive attitude, and initiative may lead to further assignments. Your child should be open about his or her job search. A temporary may be asked, "Are you new?" An example of a response is: "I'm working as a temporary in the marketing department while I look for a job in pharmaceutical sales. I recently graduated from Simmons College with a biology major."

Your child should determine how temporary work fits in with a job search strategy. A series of short-term assignments may finance day-to-day expenses and allow time to schedule interviews. Some temps work three or four days a week or for several weeks with time between assignments. Others take long-term projects of several months to learn new skills, make networking contacts, acquire references, and position themselves to hear about openings before positions are advertised.

Which candidate is more likely to penetrate the "hidden job market": the one who is paralyzed with inertia and sitting at home watching TV talk shows, or the one who works at CNN this week and IBM the next? Encourage your child to make the most of temporary work as he or she is finding the right niche.

Contract Firms

Contract firms typically differ from temporary firms in several respects. The contract firm often provides benefits for its employees, unlike many temporary firms. Contract firm work assignments tend to be longer in duration than those with temporary agencies. It is not unusual for contract employees to work for the same client for years at a time. When one assignment ends, the contract employee remains on the payroll until placed with another client. Temporaries risk intermittent periods of unemployment between assignments.

Adventure and Hospitality Jobs

Mary brought up the subject tentatively, "So, have you been doing any interviewing yet on campus?"

Her son, Tyler, dismissed the possibility out of hand. "They don't have the kind of jobs I want."

Hopeful that her son had found a sense of direction at last, Mary asked, "What kind of jobs do you want?"

"After graduation I'm planning to move to Jackson Hole, Wyoming, with two of my friends."

"What will you do out there?" Mary asked.

"I don't know, but I'm sure it will work out,"

Tyler assured her. "We'll just be gone for the summer."

The friends quickly found jobs as retail sales clerks and waiters. They thrived in their new setting, enjoying outdoor sports and social activities with recent graduates from colleges all over the country.

But summer came and went, and then, like many recent graduates, Tyler and his friends found it difficult to leave their time-off jobs for real jobs.

Your son or daughter's vision of the ideal job after graduation may center less on the position than the place. Many students dream about jobs in exotic locales: tropical islands, mountains, beaches, ranches, or cruise ships. Employers of choice may include those in tourism and adventure companies: amusement and theme parks, ski resorts, tourist submarine companies, dude ranches, safari guide companies, hot-air balloon companies, and tour escort companies.

What kinds of jobs are available for new graduates in these settings?

- **Resorts** hire front desk clerks, secretaries, accounting clerks, cooks, wait staff, gift shop clerks, lifeguards, bartenders, and bellhops. (**Ski resorts** in addition hire ski instructors, lift operators, and snowmaker operators.)

- **Amusement parks** hire singers, dancers, photographers, ride operators, animal handlers, tram operators, and admission cashiers.

- **Adventure travel companies** hire tour guides (for bicycling, whitewater rafting, kayaking, horseback riding, jet boating, etc.), photography and video staff, and food service personnel. **Hot-air balloon companies** hire balloon pilots, ground crew, and "champagne celebration hostesses."

- **Ranches** hire wranglers, campfire entertainers, ranch cooks, and farmhands.

- **Cruises** hire assistant cruise directors, disk jockeys, sound and light technicians, youth counselors, magicians, vocalists, instrumentalists, and wait staff.

If your child accepts a minimum wage job with a wait staff at a ski resort, you may be quick to point out its disadvantages: low pay, undesirable hours, poor benefits, and lack of advancement opportunities. But after taking the job, what is he or she most likely to talk about? Skiing during lunch hour. Despite your evaluation of this type of experience, your child may consider it the best time of his or her life.

It may surprise you how well your child can live on a hospitality job. One graduate reported that she made $80–130 a day in wages and tips at a ski resort restaurant. "People bring a lot of money on vacation. They're in a good mood, and they tip generously," she explained. "The job also offered special perks, such as discounted ski passes."

If your child is interested in resort, adventure, or tour escort jobs, certain skills could prove to be an advantage: CPR and Red Cross first aid certificates, bicycle repair skills, camping, tennis, skiing, horseback riding, and photography.

Many resort jobs are seasonal, such as from Memorial Day to Labor Day. Others require a commitment of eight months to two years.

Employers in these fields may limit consideration to applicants who have already relocated and can interview in person. One recent finance graduate from Seattle University works in sales for Cruiser Bob's Original Haleakala Downhill on the island of Maui, Hawaii. This unusual tour company leads bicycle trips down a volcano. Bob Kiger ("Cruiser Bob") only hires applicants who live on Maui. "Camping out on the beach" doesn't count, he notes; however, he says that it is not difficult to obtain employment in the service industry once an individual decides to move to Hawaii.

Some graduates may find their niche in the hospitality industry, which often promotes from within for management jobs. Hospitality employees who later apply for unrelated jobs may find themselves stereotyped by prospective employers. Waiting on tables or operating a cash register, no matter how glamorous the surroundings, may not be considered relevant background for jobs requiring a college degree.

Short-Term Business- and Law-Related Options

Analyst Programs

Does your child want to work for a while before continuing his or her education? For a graduate with very competitive qualifications (high GPA, internships, leadership activities), a two-year analyst position may be perfect. Investment banks and consulting firms offer these opportunities, designed for exceptional students who want a demanding job without a long-term commitment. Analyst positions are especially desirable for those who are interested in graduate business education. Some firms offer analysts job opportunities following the two-year program that do not require further education.

Analysts often enjoy the variety of working on projects that provide exposure to different departments, companies, industries, and regions. This breadth allows them greater perspective in evaluating future career decisions.

Some firms, such as Deloitte & Touche, hold an MBA Symposium to help their analysts prepare for application to top MBA programs. Analysts receive advice from predecessors who have successfully entered business school and from admissions officers.

Top-tier MBA programs actively recruit analysts for admission. These applicants typically have well-honed quantitative skills and broad exposure to problem solving for businesses in different industries.

Some employers offer tuition reimbursement to analysts who are rehired following business school.

Legal Assistant/Paralegal Work

Is your son or daughter considering a career as a lawyer? Some legal firms, district attorney's offices, and government agencies hire new bachelor's-level graduates for a year or more as legal assistants or paralegals. This provides them with exposure to the law profession and a break before beginning another three years of education.

White & Case, an international law firm based in New York, assigns legal assistants to a practice specialty, such as litigation or trust and estates. The firm asks applicants for at least a two-year commitment. The U. S. Department of Justice also offers a two-year Paralegal Program in its Antitrust Division.

Time-off experiences are so different that it is difficult to generalize about their value. One new graduate spent a year as a volunteer with Mother Theresa and found that medical schools were impressed with this unusual background and the compassion that it showed. Working as a waiter, however, whether in Paris or in Colorado Springs, is not likely to be regarded as advantageous by most employers seeking college graduates for career-track positions.

Summary

Possible Reasons for Taking Time Off

- Uncertainty about career direction

- Burnout and lack of energy for a job search or graduate school

- Desire to gain more skills or experience before beginning a job search

REASONS FOR TAKING TIME OFF
(Answer Key)

Responses 1, 4, 6, 8, 10
Consider work with a temporary service or contract firm to explore your career interests and many types of employers. You may also apply for two-year analyst positions if your background is competitive. Internships are another possibility for testing out possible career fields. If you are considering a law career, you may want to work as a legal assistant before applying to law school.

Responses 2, 5, 9
Several books such as *Jobs in Paradise* and *Now Hiring! Destination Resort Jobs,* are helpful for identifying options in hospitality or adventure fields. Is there a certain type of setting you have in mind, such as a theme park, ski resort, dude ranch, or cruise line? Can you acquire skills related to your future career goals with an employer in the location you desire? For example, someone interested in public relations may apply for jobs in guest services, sales, and other related areas.

If you feel burned out, how long do you need to recharge your batteries? Some employers will allow new graduates to take a few months off before starting work, so beware of passing up opportunities to interview during your senior year. You could graduate with a job *and* time off. Volunteer work may help you overcome burnout as you are helping others.

Responses 3, 7, 9
What kind of time commitment are you willing to make? (Some programs, such as teaching English abroad and the Peace Corps, require participants to commit to a one- or two-year period.) Do you need to earn a salary or a stipend to cover incidentals, or can you afford to pay for the experience? (You could make enough to save money while teaching English in Japan, whereas other options could require a fee up to several thousands of dollars.) Will you need to work for an agency whose volunteers qualify for deferral of college loans?

Response 6
Before you make decisions that involve sacrificing career or educational opportunities, discuss the level of commitment you and your special friend have in your relationship. (One student was prepared to limit his willingness to relocate to remain close to a girlfriend, only to learn that she was not as serious about their relationship as he was.) If you decide to stay in a particular location, consider working for a temporary service or a national company with offices where you may be able to transfer in a later move.

- Opportunity to serve through volunteer work

- A chance to test out a variety of career fields

- Time to do something fun or adventurous before taking a career position

- Desire to travel abroad to enhance cross-cultural and language skills or personal development

Evaluation of Time Off by Employers and Graduate Schools

Positive

- Enhancement of an applicant's skills and experience

- An increase in career focus

- Demonstration of a commitment to service (for nonprofits, medical schools, etc.)

Negative

- Questionable maturity and motivation

- Lack of career-related experience (depending on how the time has been spent)

- Less recognition after time for college honors

- Management training programs already filled when a graduate is ready to begin a job search

Typical Time-Off Options

- Travel, study, or work abroad

- Domestic volunteer work or internship

- Analyst programs (investment banks, consulting firms) and paralegal positions

- Adventure or hospitality industry jobs

- Nondegree study programs

- Temporary/contract work

Considerations Relating to Travel, Work, or Study Abroad

- Organization sponsorship and support services
- Health and safety; living and working conditions
- Training and orientation
- Costs/income/loan deferment/financial assistance
- Marketability/relationship to career goals
- Visa status and duration

Conversation Starters for Parents and Students

1. What are your plans immediately after graduation?

2. Why are you considering taking time off? What professional and personal goals do you have for this period?

3. How do prospective employers or graduate schools evaluate the type of experience you are considering? Do you know anyone who has recently returned from this type of experience or program?

4. What length of time are you planning to commit to this experience? (Many programs, such as teaching English abroad and the Peace Corps, require a one- or two-year commitment.)

5. How do you plan to finance this experience?

6. How will you arrange for health insurance?

CHAPTER 8

BEGINNING THE JOB SEARCH

Your child's senior year will come faster than you can imagine. (Surely it was only five or six years ago that you were teaching your son or daughter to ride a two-wheeler!) But you have your bankbook to prove that your child has indeed made it through three (or more) years of college and will soon be graduating.

While you are beginning the year with much anticipation of being tuition free (at least for this child), your child may be feeling great anxiety.

Graduating college students face a time of uncertainty unlike anything they have seen before. Not only are they unsure about what they will be doing next year, they do not know where they will be doing it, nor for whom. To make matters worse, they can't even be certain that they will find a job!

Students are aware of the competitive job market and the difficulty of finding work after graduation. They have heard the horror stories about the fraternity brother who graduated last year and is driving a pizza truck, or the young woman next door who spent eight months looking for a job and finally found one selling satellite dishes door-to-door (on straight commission).

The fear of failing can nearly paralyze students in their senior year. Students who haven't done early career planning often do not have confidence that they will succeed in the job market. They may avoid using the career office and may procrastinate about getting started on their job search until the last possible moment—perhaps only a few weeks before graduation.

We hope, though, your child has taken the advice of this book and has been preparing for a career throughout college. If so, there is every reason to believe that the job hunt will be successful, given a little realism, flexibility, and persistence.

The exercise at the end of this chapter ("Job Hunter's Reality Check") may be useful for helping your child assess his or her qualifications. It can be a good tool for the two of you to discuss at the beginning of the senior year.

(This exercise can also be helpful for a sophomore or junior, because it will indicate areas needing work.)

Where to Start

Where and when should students begin their job search?

If they have engaged in career planning as recommended, they have actually started their job search long before their senior year. Their exploration and decision making to determine their career choice; their participation in extracurricular activities, part-time jobs, and internships; and their contacts made through networking, career fairs, and professional associations have put them in a strong position to now find a job. They are already far ahead of most seniors, many of whom are just beginning some of these activities.

We recommend that students actively begin job hunting at the beginning of their senior year. In fact, some ambitious students may want to work on their résumé and cover letters and begin researching employers during the summer after their junior year. Even students who are planning to apply to graduate or professional school would be wise to pursue employment as a backup plan, since many applicants are not admitted. (By the time such applicants learn this, however, it is typically late April—often too late to begin trying to take advantage of the many interviews and other job-related opportunities offered by their campus career office. Table 8.1 gives a recommended timeline for the senior who has done the preparatory career planning work.

Many books are available on the job search; in fact, there are entire books devoted to each of the job search steps, such as writing a résumé, interviewing, and networking. In this chapter the *basics* of the job search are covered. Books are referenced in the Appendix for further reading.

The Tools

1. The Résumé

"Who am I anyway? Am I my résumé?"

So goes the line from the popular Broadway show *A Chorus Line*. To the graduating student the answer is *yes*. Generally speaking, the job hunter *is* his or her résumé, and vice versa.

The résumé represents the job hunter's qualifications to the prospective

Table 8.1

SENIOR YEAR JOB SEARCH TIMELINE

Aug/Sept	Sept/Nov	Dec/Jan	mid Jan/Mar	mid March	April/May
Draft résumé; have it critiqued by career office.	Meet with campus career counselor.	Use semester break to contact prospective employers.	Discuss progress with campus career counselor.	Prepare for and schedule second interviews if invited by employers.	Discuss progress with campus career counselor.
Print résumé.	Schedule videotaped practice interview with career counselor.	Write or call alumni and other contacts; ask for referrals.	Use other methods of job seeking (Internet, professional journals, classified ads, etc.).	Use spring break to meet with prospective employers.	Continue to contact prospective employers.
Register for and attend career office orientation.	Interview through career office.	Prepare for and schedule second interviews if invited by employers.	Continue campus interviewing.	Call helpful contacts.	Continue to network with contacts.
Attend career office workshops on interviewing and job search techniques.	Follow up with employers.		Contact referrals and follow up with previous contacts.		Discuss job offers with career counselor.
Make list of useful contacts.	Attend career fairs and panels.				

employer and should make a polished first impression. It is essential that the résumé be done well and represent the student in the best possible light.

The résumé is the most critical tool in determining whether job seekers will be granted an interview (unless the job seeker has a close contact with influence with the employer). It is the interview itself, rather than the résumé, that actually determines whether the candidate will be offered the job.

At the end of this chapter is an outline of a recommended résumé format as well as the résumés of two students—one a technical major and one a liberal arts major.

Typically the sections on a college senior's résumé include:

- Name and contact information

- Objective

- Special skills (optional)

- Education

- Honors (optional)

- Relevant course work (optional)

- Relevant experience

- Other experience

- College activities

- References

Below are 22 general rules for the résumé of a graduating student:

1. Keep the résumé to one page unless you had a number of significant work or leadership activities that require a second page.

2. Be absolutely sure that the résumé is error free (no typos or misspelled words) and is easy to read. (Use adequate spacing and type size, and highlight categories with boldface print.)

3. Use a laser printer or have the résumé typeset; use good-quality white or off-white bond paper.

4. Begin with name, address, and telephone number. Two addresses and telephone numbers (home and school) may be listed. Fax and e-mail addresses may be listed if available.

5. Do not include height, weight, date of birth, health, salary desired, or a photograph.

6. Do not include high school information unless you graduated from a prestigious private school (it is then acceptable to include the name of the school and date of graduation) or were awarded a significant honor, such as valedictorian.

7. Use an objective that is brief and to the point (e.g., "An entry-level position in market research," "A position in software development," "A position utilizing my communication and mathematical skills").

8. On a résumé that will be used through the career office, include college GPA if it is above a 2.5; for use outside the career office, include the GPA if it is above 3.0. Also include your GPA in your major if it is noticeably higher than your overall GPA (.2 or more) and if your major is relevant to your job objective.

9. List separately GPAs from different colleges attended. Do not combine them.

10. Include all academic and other honors. Briefly explain them if they are not self-explanatory, e.g., "Order of Omega (leadership honor society)."

11. List work and significant extracurricular experiences in reverse chronological order (most recent first). Begin with position title, followed by employer or organization, location (city and state), dates of employment or participation, and description of responsibilities and accomplishments. For less-significant extracurricular activities, simply list your role ("Member," "Secretary," etc.) and the name of the organization.

12. If you have two or more experiences relevant to your career goal, separate experience into sections entitled "Relevant Experience" and "Other Experience." Otherwise use one section labeled "Experience."

13. Use active verbs when describing work and extracurricular experiences. It is not necessary to describe less-significant jobs, such as waiter, bank teller, file clerk, unless you can describe how you excelled above others in the same position, the title does not adequately describe the work performed, or if these were your only jobs. Simply list these jobs with title, employer name, dates, and place of employment.

14. Do not minimize the importance of significant leadership roles in volunteer or campus organizations. Place these under "Relevant Experience" if appropriate.

15. Write the résumé in outline form, using short, staccato phrases, such as "Created publicity campaign for campus blood drive." Do not use pronouns (such as "I created . . .") or complete sentences.

16. Wherever possible specify results achieved and quantify responsibilities and results (e.g., "Raised over $10,000 for homeless shelter," "Ranked #1 among 12 salespersons for the summer," "Tutored ten students in upper-level Spanish").

17. Include special skills, such as knowledge of computer languages or software and hardware, foreign languages, and laboratory skills, in a

section entitled "Special Skills." If these are relevant to your career goals, place this section near the top of your résumé (after "Objective"). Otherwise place it near the bottom, above "References."

18. Other optional sections are "Community Activities," "Military Experience," "Publications," "Professional Associations," "Interests and Activities."

19. Be cautious about indicating religious and political affiliation on your résumé unless all of your leadership experience is with these organizations or they are related to your career goal (e.g., you have worked on a political campaign and are now applying for a job on Capitol Hill). Some employers have prejudices.

20. References should be the last item on the résumé. If there is room, list name, title, address, and telephone for three references (usually two employers and one faculty or academic adviser or administrator, or vice versa); otherwise, state, "References Available Upon Request."

21. Never put any information on your résumé that is not completely true.

22. Be careful about rounding up your GPA; a 3.29 may be rounded to a 3.3, but a 3.26 should not be. When in doubt, play it safe and give the complete GPA (3.26), or check with your career office.

Employers receive hundreds of résumés in the mail each day. IBM, for example, receives over one million résumés each year! A résumé must be perfectly done and have strong content in order to stand out.

Your son or daughter should draft a résumé and take it to the career office to be critiqued. He or she should not rely on a friend, a big brother (even if he wrote a résumé a few years ago that helped him land a job), an aunt, or you (even if you are the personnel director of a large company) to write his or her résumé.

All of these people can help with the first draft, but counselors in the career office are usually in the best position to know what most employers seek in the résumé of a new graduate. College career counselors have contact with hundreds of employers in a large variety of fields. If your child knows the personnel director of the XYZ Company and wants to work for the XYZ Company, by all means, he or she should seek advice about the résumé (and other aspects of the job search) from this contact; however, keep in mind that this person is an expert on the *XYZ Company*, not necessarily *all* companies. Some organizations have preferences that are unique to them, and a student may be given advice that will not serve well with other organizations.

Many large organizations, such as the White House, Disneyland, and Ford Motor Company, are now using optical scanners to "read" résumés into computer databases. The employer can search the database for keywords. For example, a manager who is seeking an individual with accounting skills who speaks German can search the database using "accounting" and "German" as the keywords. Résumés that will be sent to large or technical organizations that might be using optical scanners should be written and formatted somewhat differently. For example, italics and underlining should be avoided, and responsibilities should be described with nouns rather than verbs. The résumé should be printed in simple black type on white paper that is not folded or stapled. *Electronic Résumé Revolution* by Joyce Lain Kennedy and Thomas J. Morrow is an excellent book on this topic.

2. The Cover Letter

Writing a good cover letter is an important skill for anyone seeking a job. It is amazing how many well-educated job hunters do not know the correct format for a business letter! Below is an outline of the correct format. The cover letter should be typed on good-quality bond paper that matches the paper used for the résumé.

Most cover letters are mailed, although some may be deposited at the career office to be sent by the office to a particular employer. Students should mail the letter, with the résumé attached by paper clip, in a large brown envelope to avoid having to crease them.

Whenever possible the cover letter should be written to a specific person (e.g., "Dear Ms. White"). A student who does not have a contact name should make some effort to obtain one: he or she might check with the career office, the campus alumni network, or company literature and directories, or even call the organization and ask for the name of the director of human resources (sales manager, etc.). If a name cannot be located or the student is responding to a post office box listed in a classified ad, the letter should be addressed, "Dear Sir or Madam."

A cover letter should typically be about three paragraphs long and limited to one page. The content should not repeat in detail the information on the enclosed résumé but rather should highlight the information on the résumé and in the student's background that significantly relates to this specific organization (and position, if known). The letter should also indicate *why the student is interested in this particular organization* and should present a strong case for *how the student might contribute to it.*

Job hunters often mistakenly approach the cover letter from the point of view of what the organization can do for them. Although this is, of course, their primary reason for writing, they must view the cover letter and résumé as a marketing tool and indicate what they have to offer the employer. (Would a salesman try to tell you what he will gain if you buy his product?)

If the student has been referred to the employer by a particular person (perhaps Uncle Jack, who is a vice president of the organization, or the director of the career office), the student should mention this at the beginning of the letter. Employers, like most of us, tend to pay more attention to a referral from someone they know.

COVER LETTER FORMAT

22–A Summit Place
Los Angeles, CA 90049
October 10, 1996

Ms. Judith Smith
Director of Marketing
Cameron Manufacturing, Inc.
1500 Main Street
St. Louis, MO 63124

Dear Ms. Smith:

(Opening paragraph) State why you are writing, name the position or type of work for which you are applying, and mention how you heard about the opening or the organization.

(Middle paragraph) Explain why you are interested in working for THIS employer, and specify your reasons for desiring this type of work. If you have had experience, be sure to point out your particular achievements or other qualifications that make you a strong candidate. Refer the reader to the enclosed résumé, and restate a few of the most pertinent points on your résumé.

(Closing paragraph) Indicate that you wish to meet with the employer to discuss your qualifications, and state that you will be contacting the employer by telephone within a week. Also, give the employer information about how to contact you should he or she desire.

Sincerely,

(Signature)

Sara A. Brown

enclosure: résumé

Although most job hunters will draft a basic cover letter, it must be individualized for each employer so that it reads as if it were written specifically for that organization. The organization's name should appear in the letter (e.g., "I am very eager to work for Nike," rather than, "I am very eager to work for your organization"), and the letter should contain several sentences indicating that the writer has researched the organization and knows something about it.

Students should close their letter by stating that they will be contacting the employer within a week to discuss their application. (Obviously they must then do so!) This approach is more impressive than the typical passive one of asking to be contacted if the employer has interest. It also enables the student to get some quick feedback from the employer since it does not put the student in the position of waiting for the employer's response—which may never come!

Students should have one or two of their cover letters reviewed by a career counselor before sending them. Obviously there should be no grammatical or spelling errors.

3. The Interview

The interview is the most important step of the job search process. Often a college student's first interview will be with an employer on campus. If the employer has further interest, the student will usually be invited at the employer's expense for a second interview, often called an "on-site" interview, generally conducted at the employer's location. Whether the interview is on campus, at the employer's facility, or elsewhere, preparation is essentially the same: The student must research the organization. The student who is applying for a particular position should learn as much about it as possible. He or she should prepare both answers to questions the employer might ask and questions to ask the employer.

Interview Preparation

Students often underestimate the need for employer and industry research; they may go into the interview having done little or no preparation, thinking that they will be able to "wing it." Employers, however, can easily spot those students who have not prepared and will generally eliminate them from further consideration.

Many resources exist to help students with their research. Employers interviewing on campus almost always send company literature and sometimes provide videotapes or computer diskettes to the career office for student use. Students contacting employers who are not visiting campus should also check with the career office for information. If none is available, they might write or call the organization and request company literature.

The campus library has many directories, such as *Moody's* and *Standard & Poor's* corporate directories, that have information on most large organizations.

Students interested in particular industries should read professional publications in those fields, such as *Advertising Age* or *Computerworld*. Since many jobs are in the business world, it is a good idea for students to read at least one business publication on a regular basis, such as the *Wall Street Journal, Fortune, Business Week*, or *Forbes*.

Many companies now have information about their organization, including employment information, available on the Internet. If students are familiar with the Internet, they can use a "search engine" to seek information on a particular organization.

Contacting friends, former classmates, and alumni who work in the targeted organization or industry is another way to obtain information.

Students should have a good idea of what they want to do for the organization to which they are applying. "I'll do anything" is neither an acceptable nor an honest answer. (Will they really come in at 4:00 A.M. to sweep the floors?) They do not necessarily have to identify a specific job title, but they should be at least able to discuss the skills they have and are interested in using. They might say, for example, "I've always been able to easily establish rapport with people, and I have good communication skills. I am interested in a job in sales"; or, "I am interested in a job that will allow me to use my computer and mathematical skills and my strong analytic ability."

Although employers often want candidates with good interpersonal skills, they hear the phrase "I want to work with people" so often that they dislike it intensely! Job hunters should avoid it.

In addition to having knowledge about the particular organization (and job, if possible), students should have at least a basic understanding of the industry to which they are applying. If interviewing with a textile company, they should read about the textile industry; if applying to a bank, they should know about the various entry-level positions in banking and something about banking in general (including the current prime rate!). It is also important to know who the organization's competitors are.

Preparing for the interview includes rehearsing answers to questions that employers are likely to ask. At the end of this chapter is a list of questions that employers frequently ask college seniors and new graduates. Many employers now use an interview approach called targeted selection, or behavioral interviewing. In this type of interview, the employer is seeking examples of specific behavior that relates to particular traits desired. For example, rather than directly asking the student if he or she is creative or has leadership qualities, the interviewer will ask the student, "Give me an example of a time you came up with an innovative approach to a difficult problem," or "Tell me about a time when you exhibited leadership skills."

Before their interviews students should think about several "war stories" they might tell to demonstrate various traits like leadership, creativity, high achievement, handling failure, and teamwork. They might write these down or rehearse articulating them to you or a friend. Most career offices offer students the opportunity to have a "mock," or practice, interview, which can be videotaped. After the interview the career counselor critiques the student's verbal and nonverbal behavior. This service is extremely helpful and should be used if available.

Students should prepare questions to ask the employer in order to show interest in the organization and the job. Questions might arise from recent news stories about the organization or might be about the training program, advancement opportunities, or attrition rate. Questions about salary and benefits should not be asked; the employer should introduce these subjects first, usually at the offer stage.

Interview Attire

In general, students should dress conservatively for an interview. Males should wear a navy or charcoal gray suit with a white long-sleeve dress shirt and a traditional tie. A sport coat and slacks are too casual for most interviews. They should wear dark socks (long enough to cover their leg when crossed!) And well-polished black dress shoes. Their hair should be neatly cut. It is strongly advised that they have no facial hair; however, if they choose to have a beard or mustache, it must be immaculately groomed.

For most industries, a conservative haircut (no Mohawks or ponytails) is recommended. The only jewelry acceptable is a watch and a class or signet ring or a wedding band. (No gold chains or diamond earrings, please!)

Females should wear a suit (matching jacket and skirt—no pants) in a conservative color or muted pattern. Recommended colors are black, navy, gray, burgundy, dark green, and camel. They should wear nude-colored hose and polished, close-toed pumps with a medium-height heel. If they choose to bring a handbag to the interview, it should coordinate with their outfit and not be oversized. Women should keep jewelry to a minimum (not more than one earring for each ear and no more than a total of three rings on their hands). Long hair should be worn up or held back off the face with a clip.

Students interviewing for positions in artistic, creative, or high-fashion fields should show more personal flair and fashion awareness in their dress.

Good interview clothes are expensive, costing about $300—500 for the complete outfit. Help your son or daughter budget for this in advance, so neither of you will be caught off guard when it is time to purchase it. (Perhaps this could be a birthday, holiday, or graduation gift.)

Students may want to bring a leather or simulated-leather portfolio with paper and a pen to the interview to take occasional notes. (A briefcase is too formal and bulky.) They may use the pen and paper to take a few notes (such as a date to contact the employer or a name and address referred by the employer), but they should avoid writing throughout the interview. They should also bring extra copies of their résumé and a list of their references (with contact information) if the references are not listed on their résumé.

Students also might want to bring samples of their work, if available and relevant for their career field. For example, students interested in advertising should bring a portfolio with some of the campaigns they developed; those seeking positions involving writing should bring clippings of published work.

The Interview Itself

Students should plan to arrive for the interview about ten minutes early. If the interview is on campus, it is wise to know ahead of time in which building and room the interview will be held. If the interview is at the employer's office or another facility, it is helpful to go there on an earlier day to ensure that it can be found easily. It is the kiss of death to show up late for an interview! If, however, unforeseen circumstances occur—such as a flat tire—that cause a delay, it is essential that the student call and explain the reason for being late.

Some employers also strongly object to an applicant's arriving *too early* for a scheduled interview. So a student who is interviewing at the employer's location and who arrives more than 10 to 15 minutes ahead of time should walk or drive around the block a few times before announcing his or her arrival.

Students should enter the interview room with an air of confidence (but not cockiness). They should greet the interviewer by name and with a handshake. Young women, in particular, are often not yet accustomed to shaking hands. Students should practice a firm handshake. Inserting the web of their hand (between the forefinger and thumb) into the web of the interviewer's hand will ensure that their handshake is firm and not "fishy"—a pet peeve of most employers.

Students should take an active part in the interview. They should appear animated and enthusiastic. Their answers should be long enough to cover the subject without boring the interviewer. (When the recruiter's eyes begin to glaze over, it's time to stop!) As discussed above, they should give concrete examples that relate to the employer's questions. An easy-to-remember formula is to use the *BAR* approach: that is, when giving an example they should first give the *Background* of the situation, then the *Action* that they took, and finish with the *Result* that occurred.

The student should be sensitive to the interviewer's cues. It is the employer who should lead the interview, setting the pace for the student to elaborate on a response to a question or to move on to the next item. If unsure about how much detail to give, the student should give a fairly brief answer and ask whether the employer would like more information.

If a student is confronted with a particularly difficult question, it is acceptable to take a moment or two to think before responding. It is far better to wait a few seconds, saying something like, "I'd like to think about that for a moment," than to blurt out a quick answer that the student will regret, or to ask to come back to it later (since the employer will probably forget).

Basically the interviewer is seeking to learn whether the student 1) will be able to do the job, 2) will be promotable, 3) will have a positive attitude, and 4) will fit in with the corporate culture. The more preparation the student does before the interview, the better he or she will be able to convince the interviewer of these four things.

Students must not only strive to impress the employer with their verbal responses, they must also be aware of their nonverbal behavior, or "body language." Nervous habits, such as twisting a ring, tapping a pencil, or crossing and uncrossing legs, are distracting to the interviewer. Students should avoid sitting too far forward, very stiffly, or with their hands folded across the chest; on the other hand, a position that is too relaxed comes across as cocky and arrogant. They should make eye contact with the interviewer but should not stare. (Looking at the interviewer's forehead rather than directly in the eye can ensure this.)

Videotaped practice interviews allow students to observe and receive coaching on both their verbal and nonverbal interview behavior.

At the close of the interview, the student should shake the employer's hand and thank him or her for the interview. If the student is still interested in the opportunity, it is important to *clearly state that he or she wants the job and ask the employer to hire him or her for it.* (This feels quite awkward to most students, but it is recommended time and again by employers—especially those recruiting for sales positions. Many employers state that this can be the distinguishing factor that determines which students will be offered second interviews.) The student might say, for example, "Ms. Thomas, I am very interested in working for The Widget Company, and I believe that my background is a good fit for this position. I hope you will hire me."

Here are some additional pointers for students regarding the interview:

- Do not denigrate current or former employers or teachers.

- Take an active part in the interview! Be prepared with good questions as well as good answers.

- If the employer hasn't asked about a particular strength or significant experience, find a way to discuss it before the close of the interview (e.g., "There is one more thing I'd like to add before we finish, if I may. . . .").

- Be prepared to discuss weaknesses as well as strengths (a favorite question of many employers), but try to indicate how you are overcoming your weaknesses. Do not volunteer weaknesses, however.

- Do not ask about salary or benefits during the first interview, but have some idea of the appropriate salary range for the position in case you are asked about salary expectations. This information may be obtained from the career office.

- Ask when you might expect to hear further from the employer, if he or she has not indicated a time frame.

The Follow-Up

Some job seekers have an excellent interview and then shoot themselves in the foot by not following up afterward. What does follow-up involve?

Obviously students should provide the employer with anything requested in the interview. For example, the employer may have asked the student to call the employer's office to arrange to take some type of test, or the employer may have requested that the student have a transcript forwarded by the registrar. These activities should be completed as soon as possible after the interview. Also, students should always send a typed letter within three days of the interview thanking the employer for his or her time and expressing continued interest in the organization and position.

If the student has not heard from the employer within a week or two after the time indicated, the student should call the employer to show interest and ask whether any decision has been made. Unless the student is discouraged from contacting the employer or has received a rejection letter, it may be good to drop a brief note (typed) or phone the employer every six weeks or so to stay in touch.

Second Interviews

Students who have interviewed on campus and have successfully made it through the first cut or screening will usually be invited to a second, or even third, interview before a final hiring decision is made. Depending on the employer and the position, these additional interviews may be conducted in the career office, may involve "a day in the field" (during which the student accompanies an employee, such as a sales representative, on the job for a day), or may be scheduled at a regional or corporate office.

Second interviews may involve taking one or more tests that measure an individual's likelihood of success in the position or field. A student may be brought to an organization along with other students whom the employer is considering, and he or she may be asked to participate in several group activities. In these activities the employer is observing the interaction among the students in order to assess an individual's leadership ability as well as teamwork. A student will generally be interviewed by several managers, either individually or in a small group, at a second interview.

Generally the employer will cover all reasonable expenses associated with the second interview. If this has not been stated by the employer, the student should tactfully ask for clarification in advance. ("May I assume that you will be reimbursing me for my expenses?") Most students cannot afford to pay for these (and most parents do not want to!).

Students will probably need a credit card to initially charge travel expenses for second interviews; often reimbursement is made by check a few weeks later. Also, many students do not realize the need for traveling with sufficient cash. If they are interviewing in large cities, like New York or Chicago, they should take a credit card plus a minimum of $100 cash for two days to pay for taxis, phone calls, tips, and other miscellaneous expenses.

Students should use good judgment when incurring costs. Occasionally students yield to the temptation of living "high on the hog" on a temporary expense account, and some are simply naive about what is appropriate. One unfortunate student did not realize that the food and drinks stocked in the minibar of a posh hotel were not free; the evening before his interview, he invited some of his friends in the area to join him for a party in his room. When he left the city, his room charge, paid by the employer, included a $150 minibar tab! The employer paid the bill but informed the director of his career office that the student had just eliminated himself from consideration for a highly prestigious and lucrative job offer. Moral of the story: when in doubt, do not charge it to the employer!

As with the first interview, the student should send a typed follow-up letter within three days of a second interview. If the student has met with several people, he or she can write to all of them or write to the one or two key individuals and mention the others in the letters.

4. Networking

Job hunting is a contact sport! Throughout this book the importance of making contacts has been stressed. These contacts will be extremely useful to students as they begin their job search.

You can help your son or daughter brainstorm to develop a list of all of the people you both know who might be able to assist. The list should include the obvious relatives, neighbors, friends, and coworkers but should also extend to your child's classmates, teachers, advisers, guest lecturers, and contacts made through participating in career programs, extracurricular activities, and internships and cooperative education experiences.

The concept of networking is, however, much more extensive than using existing contacts. It means making a concerted effort to expand one's immediate circle of contacts. Active participation in student professional associations (including attending conferences if students are allowed), use of the campus alumni connections, and seeking professionals employed in fields of interest are some ways of doing this.

Students often underestimate their circle of contacts. When asked about their contacts who could be helpful, they generally answer "no one" or come up with a very small list. However, after prodding and coaching, they are astonished to realize how many possible contacts they actually have.

Like most job seekers, students limit their thinking to their "first-level" contacts. That is, they think that in order to get help, they must know a contact who will *directly* lead to a job. However, research shows that it is usually a third- or fourth-level contact who actually results in a job. The source of the job is usually not the person the job hunter knows but the person who knows the person who knows the person the job hunter knows!

Imagine a bull's-eye, with a student's first-level contacts in the ring immediately adjacent to the bull's-eye. When the student asks these contacts for referrals he or she meets the contacts in the next ring. Asking these second-level contacts for referrals makes contacts in the next ring, or third-level, and so forth. And it is these third- and fourth-level contacts—people the student never knew at the start of the process—who are most likely to be the ones that can lead to a job.

When Liz began seeking a job in publishing, she used many avenues. She took advantage of the opportunities that were available through her career office, but few publishers were recruiting on campus. She used the career office, however, to obtain contact information for many publishers, to which she sent cover letters and her résumé. She also spoke to as many people as possible about her desire to find work in the publishing field, preferably as an editorial assistant.

One of the people to whom Liz spoke was a man who had made a presentation at a career panel sponsored by her career office. He indicated that he did not anticipate any opening in his organization, since they were currently going through a downsizing, but he gave Liz the name of a colleague of his at another publishing company whom he thought might be doing some hiring.

Liz contacted this woman, who in turn, told Liz that her organization was not hiring anyone; but she suggested that Liz get in touch with a friend of hers who had recently become editor of a small start-up magazine and was looking for a few entry-level people. Liz called the editor, who requested her résumé. A few weeks later Liz interviewed with the editor and shortly thereafter was hired!

It is important for students to let virtually every one of their contacts know that they are graduating soon and seeking assistance finding a job. Students sometimes are a bit proud about asking for help, or they worry that if they obtain a job through a connection, they will be looked upon as someone who couldn't find a job on their own. But there is nothing at all wrong with using contacts in a job search; in fact, that is the way most people make the initial contact with their employer.

Students should send a brief typewritten note to each contact used to thank them for their assistance. They should also let them know which job they eventually accept and try to reciprocate in some way.

To spread the word about their job search, some students have business cards printed with their name and contact information and a very brief summary of their credentials. This gives them something easy to carry and distribute at all times in case they meet someone on an airplane, at a conference, or elsewhere. Of course, they should also have plenty of résumés on hand, too.

One creative student seeking a position in advertising even had a T-shirt and a bumper sticker for his car printed, advertising his availability! An advertising executive saw it, was impressed with his originality, and hired him!

Developing a Strategy

"Cheshire Puss," [said Alice] ". . . would you tell me, please, which way I ought to go from here?"

"That depends a good deal on where you want to get to," said the Cat.

"I don't much care where—" said Alice.

"Then it doesn't matter which way you go," said the Cat.

"—so long as I get somewhere," Alice added as an explanation.

"Oh, you're sure to do that," said the Cat, "if you only walk long enough."

—Lewis Carroll, *Alice's Adventure in Wonderland*

A senior who has been planning ahead should now have a relatively clear focus on his or her initial career goals. This is key to a successful job search; otherwise, a student, like any unfocused job hunter, will spend a lot of time on activity that is not likely to pay off with satisfying results.

If your son or daughter does not yet have a career direction—or at least a general idea of the type of work he or she wants to do, we recommend returning to some of the suggestions in Chapter 1 regarding career exploration.

Assuming that your senior is ready to move forward on the job search, a written plan of action is recommended. At the end of this chapter is a Senior Job Search Plan Worksheet to help your son or daughter develop his or her own timeline. Although there are some general rules of thumb for most seniors, the time frame of specific activities will vary depending on the individual's career field and prior preparation. The advantages of actually sitting down and writing out a job search plan are that 1) breaking down the process into discrete steps makes it appear more manageable, and 2) committing goals to paper results in a greater likelihood of follow-through.

Too many students procrastinate about their job search until late in their senior year, resulting in many missed opportunities.

Finding a job is a job in itself, and it takes time. Unless a student is going to work for a relative or has a job offer from a co-op or internship experience (which he or she plans to accept), the job search will probably take many hours. If possible, it is a good idea for a student to plan a fairly light course load during the senior year to allow the necessary time for job hunting.

Seniors should plan a job search strategy that involves activities both in and outside of their career office. They should use directories (both printed and electronic) to make lists of potential employers in their field of interest. Using their web of contacts, they should attempt to find at least one (preferably several) contact in each organization of interest. They then need to get in touch with their contacts and request help. The help they would most likely need is with information about the organization, tips for getting their foot in the door, names of appropriate contacts within the organization to inquire about entry-level positions, and assistance with obtaining an interview.

Students should set goals for the number of contacts and the number of employers they will write or call each week. It is important for job hunters to set goals and stick with them in order not to lose momentum.

After some initial letters have been mailed to employers, job seekers need to follow up by calling the employers, inquiring whether the letter has been received and, if so, asking for an interview. As mentioned above, it is the interview rather than the résumé that leads to a job. (Of course, often the résumé leads to an interview.) Therefore, the student's goal should be to obtain as many interviews with prospective employers in fields of interest as possible.

When contacting employers who do not readily agree to an interview, a bit of persistence—without being obnoxious—can often lead to a face-to-face meeting. For example, if the employer says, "We have no openings right now," the student might reply, "I understand that, but I would still like to meet with you for a short time in order to learn more about Company X; I am very interested in working for Company X, and perhaps there will be openings in the future." Although this will not always result in an interview, sometimes it will pay off; in any case the student has impressed the employer with his or her tenacity and interest in the organization.

Most employers are reluctant to agree to an interview if a student is some distance away, since there is usually the assumption that the employer will pay the travel costs. A student who is particularly interested in the employer or in a geographic region might plan (and pay for) a trip to the area and notify employers in advance that he or she will be there during a certain time period. Employers are often receptive to seeing students whose credentials are of interest under these circumstances.

Students should use as many methods of searching for a job as possible and should use all resources available to them. Often students limit themselves to one or two methods; usually campus interviews and the classified ads. Although many students find a job through campus interviews (it varies greatly by major and career field, but the national average is about 21 percent), they cannot depend on finding a job this way; and few students are successful with the classified ads, since jobs posted in the classifieds often require several years of experience and result in hundreds of responses.

In the popular job search book *What Color Is Your Parachute?* author Richard Bolles cites the following success rates for various job-hunting methods:

Using personal contacts	68.0%
Applying directly to an employer in person	47.7%
Asking friends for job leads	34.0%
Asking relatives for job leads	26.7%
Going to private employment agencies	24.2–5%*
Answering local newspaper ads	24.0–5%*
Going to a union hiring hall (for those who belong)	22.2%*
Using the campus career office	21.4%
Contracting an executive search firm	15.0%*
Using the federal/state employment service	13.7%
Placing ads yourself	12.9%
Taking federal exams	12.5%
Asking a professor or teacher for job leads	12.1%
Answering ads from nonlocal newspapers	10.0%*
Going to noncampus job fairs	8.2%
Mailing out résumés "by the bushel"	8.0%
Answering ads in journals for your field	7.3%
Using computerized listings, or "registers"	4.0%

* Indicates methods that are not options or are less successful for entry-level positions.

Reviewing these success rates makes the importance of networking evident. It also reveals, however, that although some methods are more likely to produce results than others, each method has been successful for someone. You may be sure that the four people out of a hundred who found a job through a computerized listing will swear by this method! Since it is not possible to predict which technique will work for any particular individual, the more techniques used, the greater the chance for success.

Job-Hunting Tips

All job hunters want to succeed, yet the degree of success varies tremendously. Why?

Qualifications, the chosen career field, and the amount of career planning activities account for some of the differences, but other important factors are the time, effort, and quality of effort put forth in the job search.

Here are 15 important tips for students looking for a job:

1. Make sure your résumé and cover letter look like they could be published! They must be free of typographic, spelling, and grammatical errors and be laser-printed or typeset on good-quality paper. Do not make extra copies on an inexpensive duplicating machine. Have them professionally done by a copy center. Employers consider your résumé and cover letter an example of your best effort; if they are sloppy, the employer assumes that your work, if you were hired, would be sloppy too.

2. Change the message on your answering machine from "Leave your number if you want to party tonight!" to something more appropriate; employers may be calling when you are not in. Make sure your roommate knows how important it is to pass on messages from employers accurately and promptly.

3. Be immaculately groomed when interviewing. One employer stated to the director of a career office, "When I'm interviewing a candidate, I assume that this is the best he will ever look. It will be downhill from here on."

4. Always prepare thoroughly for interviews; appear eager and interested in the jobs for which you interview.

5. If you are interested in enrolling in graduate or professional school at some time in the future, don't mention it in your interview unless you know that the employer encourages it for advancement; employers do not want to invest time and money in training you to have you leave after a short period of time.

6. Follow up promptly on all correspondence—whether it is a thank-you letter after an interview, an invitation for an on-site visit, or a job offer. (Even if you are rejecting an offer, do it promptly; you never know when you might want to reapply to that organization.)

7. Take advantage of every opportunity you have for face-to-face meetings with employers, even those in whom you have only a mild level of interest. You may learn that a position is more of a fit than you expected.

8. Brush up on your table manners and on business protocol. The interviewing process often involves business meals, cocktail parties, social events, making introductions, and other situations that require business etiquette. (See the Appendix for reference books.)

9. Be as flexible as possible about the position, the size and type of employer, and the place of employment you will consider. Many students eliminate excellent opportunities because they do not want to leave their home or college town or want to be near a "special friend." Although this is a choice you have the right to make, you must understand that you may be sacrificing your career (at least initially) for that choice. Other students do not even explore job possibilities with employers whom they do not consider prestigious. (When they are still unemployed four months later, they regret passing up that chance they had to enter a management training program.)

10. Do not overlook opportunities with small organizations. In a recent survey conducted by Dun & Bradstreet, it was predicted that three million jobs would be created in 1995; and of these jobs, 66 percent were expected to be created by firms with fewer than 100 employees. The nation's largest organizations—those with over 5,000 employees—were expected to create only 5 percent of the new jobs.

11. Set your priorities at the beginning of your job search. Few employees can have it all, especially when they are just beginning their career. Determine what is most important to you (such as a challenging job, prestigious employer, high salary, or location), and then go after it.

12. Try to devote some time each day to your job search. Plan to spend 10 to 15 hours a week on it. Do not let a week pass without doing something to further your chances of finding work.

13. Do not relax after applying or interviewing with several employers— even if you feel positive about your chance for a job offer. Many times the offer does not come through. After interviewing and doing the necessary follow-through, assume that you will *not* receive the job offer, and continue actively pursuing other possibilities.

14. Take advantage of the wealth of information about job hunting, companies, and employment opportunities listed on the Internet. If you do not know how to access the Internet, now is the time to learn! Check with your computer labs, library, or career office for assistance. Two of the best Internet sources for job hunters are at http://www.jobweb.org/catapult/catapult.html) and (http://www.wpi.edu/~mfriley/jobguide.html).

15. If all else fails, consider temporary employment or volunteer work that will allow you to develop your skills or to get a foot in the door with an employer of interest, or preferably both. In a survey by Office Team, 80 percent of executives responded that they believe it is valuable to hire someone first as a temporary worker, and 78 percent believe that consistent temporary work is comparable to full-time work.

Evaluating the Job Offer

Your son or daughter may be among the fortunate students who not only have a job offer but actually have several from which to choose. A fairly common problem for some students with good credentials who have worked hard at their job search is that of "a bird in the hand versus two in the bush."

In other words they have an offer from Company X, but they would prefer to work for Company Y, with whom they have interviewed but from whom they have not yet heard. In this situation the student should try to stall Company X by saying something like, "I am very excited about your offer and am pleased that you are interested in hiring me. I am sure that you can appreciate what an important decision this is for me, and I want to be certain that I am making the right one. I would like a bit more time to consider your offer. When do you need your final answer?"

If the job offer has been made to the student early in the senior year—before February—the student has more bargaining power in terms of time; usually the employer will allow until March or so to give a final answer. However, the later it is in the school year, the more eager the recruiter is to fill the position, and the more worried she is about losing the best backup candidates if the student is allowed too long an extension. Even late in the year, though, an employer will typically give a student at least two to three weeks to make a decision.

Students in this position should definitely contact other employers with whom they have interviewed and for whom they would prefer to work and let them know of the pending offer. Students must do this in a tactful way so that it does not appear as though they are trying to play one employer against the other or pressure a preferred employer into hiring. Nevertheless, it is appropriate for a student to call the preferred employer, explain that there is an offer to which the student must respond by a particular date, and ask if this employer might possibly be able to make a hiring decision by that date. The student should indicate that this employer is his or her first choice, if that is the case. This strategy often is successful in allowing the student to know what his or her options are before making a final decision.

There is no easy formula for determining whether a student should accept a job offer. Prior to interviewing, the student should have researched the field well enough to have a sense of the general salary range, benefits, and working conditions typical for the industry, although these will vary by size of employer, geographic region, and other factors. A student who receives an offer that he or she thinks is inappropriate, because of a very low salary, unreasonable working conditions, or other job considerations, should discuss the offer with a counselor in the career office. The counselor can advise him or her about whether to attempt to negotiate with the employer and, if so, how best to approach it.

When considering an offer, students must take into account how likely they are to receive other offers if they decline this one, how flexible they are in terms of location, salary, and other job considerations, and how much longer they can afford to continue the job search. They should discuss these issues as well with a counselor in the career office.

Some factors to consider before accepting a job offer are:

- Job responsibilities

- Training (both initial and ongoing)

- Salary (and cost of living in geographic area)

- Benefits (including educational assistance)

- Working conditions

- Lifestyle required (e.g., dress code, working hours, travel)

- Work colleagues (peers and upper management)

A student should carefully weigh a job offer before accepting it. It is considered unethical to accept a job offer and then renege, or back out of the offer, later. Not only is this bad form, it can have negative consequences: the decision may come back to haunt the student, since circles, particularly in some fields, are quite small. The employer with whom a job hunter broke faith today may become his or her boss next year or may be an organization to which he or she wants to apply in five years. And one who reneges may also be denied future use of the career office if the offer was obtained through their services.

Parental Support

How can you as a parent be supportive without being too indulgent? How do you ensure that your son or daughter is doing the necessary job search activity without nagging him or her? It is not easy—but being a parent is not easy. (You already know that!)

Many seniors begin the year enthusiastically seeking a job. But their motivation wanes about halfway through the year, as they realize how much time is involved and how frustrating rejection can be. They often give up at this point, convincing themselves that they will have more time to spend on their job search after graduation. This is a mistake. Interviews are far easier to obtain (though admittedly harder to find time for) while still in school. And employers who are contacted after graduation inevitably want to know why students did not contact them earlier. (They also may have their training classes filled by then.)

When your child becomes discouraged and convinced that "all of this time spent interviewing on campus and contacting employers off campus is useless," remind him or her that it is important to keep working at the job search.

Help your son or daughter keep on track by showing that you are interested in the progress of his or her job search (but not worried about it). When your child is disappointed by the inevitable rejection letters, remain positive. Help him or her realize that almost all students are rejected by some employers and that with persistence, a good job offer is likely to come along.

If your child has put in an adequate amount of time and effort during senior year (and has done the prerequisite early career planning), there may be a job offer by graduation, or at least several good possibilities pending. If not, continue to provide encouragement and suggestions—one of which should be for your child to stay in touch with the career office and leave plenty of résumés with them.

It is important that your expectations be realistic. In *U.S. News & World Report's America's Best Colleges: 1994 Annual Guide*, it was reported that fewer than 20 percent of the previous spring's bachelor's degree graduates had full-time jobs by graduation. Although the job market has improved somewhat, that figure has not increased significantly. (The *good* news is that approximately 95 percent of new college graduates are employed within a year of graduation.)

Let your child know that you understand that he or she may not be employed by graduation, and provide your child with emotional (and some financial, if possible) support. We do not recommend, however, unconditional and unlimited support: in a positive manner, talk with your child about using the career office, ask which employers he or she has contacted, and ask how he or she is using networking to aid in the job hunt.

If your child does not have a job and chooses (with your permission) to return home, discuss the conditions beforehand. You may want to make some new rules now that your child is no longer a guest visiting only for the holidays and an occasional weekend. Perhaps he or she should do some chores in exchange for room and board. You also may want to discuss your expectations about staying out late or informing you of his or her coming and going. Both you and your child have probably changed significantly during the college years (your child probably more than you). It can be a challenge having an adult child living at home, especially one that you are supporting financially, but setting some ground rules can ease the adjustment for all parties.

Although the particular ground rules are between you and your child, we strongly recommend that one of them be that he or she continue to work on the job search and make daily effort toward it. You also might consider asking him or her to take a part-time or temporary job in order to contribute toward expenses. (But keep in mind that constantly working in an unrelated area will neither help your child gain entry into a chosen field nor allow for time to seek employment.)

JOB HUNTER'S REALITY CHECK

This exercise can help determine how strong a student's qualifications are at a particular point in time to enter the job market. Students should discuss with a career counselor ways to increase strength in areas where scores are low. Instructions:

1. For each category, place a check mark on the line which best describes your situation. If you are unsure about some information (e.g., whether your major is high or low demand), talk with a career counselor.

2. After you have placed a check mark on a line for all items, bring the number ("score") below the line over to the far right column.

3. Total all points and refer to scoring scale below.

				# OF POINTS
• MAJOR	HIGH DEMAND 10	NEUTRAL 3	LOW DEMAND 0	_____
• CAREER GOAL	HIGH DEMAND FOR EMPLOYEES 10	RELATIVELY EQUAL BALANCE BETWEEN SUPPLY & DEMAND 3	LOW DEMAND FOR EMPLOYEES—FEW OPENINGS; VERY COMPETITIVE 0	UNSURE OF MY CAREER GOAL 0
• GRADES	OUTSTANDING (3.5 & ABOVE) 5	EXCELLENT (3.0–3.49) 4	AVERAGE (2.6–2.99) 2	NOT MY STRONG POINT (2.0–2.59) 0

continued

• WORK EXPERIENCE *RELATED* TO MY CAREER GOAL (CAN BE PAID OR UNPAID)	EXCELLENT (SEVERAL JOBS/INTERNSHIPS/ PROJECTS/CO-OP VOLUNTEER EXPERIENCES) 8	GOOD (1-2 RELATED EXPERIENCES) 5	WEAK (NO RELEVANT EXPERIENCE) 0	UNSURE OF MY CAREER GOAL 0	
• OTHER (LESS RELEVANT) WORK EXPERIENCE (PAID OR UNPAID)	EXTENSIVE (3-4 JOBS) 3	MODERATE (1-2 JOBS) 1	NONE 0		
• LEADERSHIP ROLES	EXTENSIVE (E.G., ELECTED OFFICER OF STUDENT GROUPS, SUPERVISORY EXPERIENCE ON THE JOB, ETC.) 3	GOOD-MODERATE (E.G., CHAIR OF COMMITTEES OR STUDENT GROUPS) 4	LITTLE-NONE 0		
• SPORTS ACTIVITIES	OUTSTANDING (TEAM CAPTAIN OF VARSITY SPORTS 2-4 YEARS, SPORTS HONOR ROLL, MVP IN CONFERENCE, ETC.) 4	EXCELLENT (VARSITY LESS THAN 2 YEARS, JV, CLUB SPORTS, ETC.) 3	GOOD (INTRAMURALS, SOLO SPORTS—GOLF, TENNIS, JOGGING, ETC.) 2	LITTLE-NONE 0	
• MARKETABLE SKILLS (COMPUTER, ACCOUNTING, LABORATORY, ETC.)	EXTENSIVE 8	GOOD-MODERATE 5	LITTLE-NONE 0		

continued

- INTERPERSONAL SKILLS (COMFORT LEVEL MEETING/ TALKING/ WORKING WITH PEOPLE)

| VERY COMFORTABLE 5 | SOMEWHAT COMFORTABLE 2 | GENERALLY UNCOMFORTABLE 0 | _____ |

- SOURCE OF COLLEGE DEGREE

| VERY PRESTIGIOUS/ SELECTIVE SCHOOL 5 | SCHOOL WITH GOOD ACADEMIC REPUTATION 3 | LESSER-KNOWN COLLEGE/UNIVERSITY 1 | _____ |

- "WILD CARD"—YOU MAY GIVE YOURSELF 3–6 POINTS IF YOU HAVE ADDITIONAL QUALITIES/SKILLS/FACTORS THAT ENHANCE YOUR CREDENTIALS (E.G., FINANCED 75–100% OF COLLEGE EDUCATION; STRONG NETWORK OF CONTACTS IN DESIRED FIELD; SPECIAL HONORS)

OPTIONAL 3—6 _____

TOTAL # OF POINTS _____

SCORING SCALE:

66–46   Congratulations! You've prepared well and are highly competitive. Nevertheless, in today's job market even students with the best credentials need to work hard at finding a job.

45–25   Your credentials to compete for a job are good to moderate. Be thorough and persistent about all aspects of your job search. Don't overlook opportunities to work for smaller, lesser-known organizations. Use informal contacts at career fairs and panels to impress recruiters with your interpersonal skills, since your résumé may not be strong enough to get the interviews you desire.

24–0   Your credentials in the job market are not especially strong. You may want to "beef them up" by taking some course work in areas sought by employers (e.g., accounting, business, or computer science), obtaining part-time work (either paid or unpaid) or involving yourself in campus organizations. Plan to put extra effort into your job search, and don't concentrate on prestigious employers. (Many less glamorous jobs and organizations offer excellent training opportunities.)

GENERAL FORMAT FOR A RÉSUMÉ— UNDERGRADUATE

Name
e-mail address (if available)

School Address	**Home Address**
Phone (including area code)	**Phone** (including area code)
(until date)	

OBJECTIVE (example: "A management trainee position in banking")

EDUCATION (Include all colleges attended. You may list in reverse chronological order.)

School, Place
Degree, Major, Date
Secondary concentration, option, or track

GPA: overall
      major (include only if higher than overall)
Honors:
Relevant courses: (optional)

EXPERIENCE (in reverse chronological order)

(paid, unpaid, volunteer, community services, course projects relevant to job objectives; may include summer jobs, internships, part-time jobs, college activities, cooperative education experiences, etc.)

Title, Organization Name, Location, Dates
- (list responsibilities, using action verbs, staccato phrases—do not use complete sentences)

Title, Organization Name, Location, Dates
-

Title, Organization Name, Location, Dates
-

OTHER EXPERIENCE (less-important work, summer jobs, part-time work—may summarize rather than list separately)

COLLEGE ACTIVITIES Organization, level of responsibility, dates of involvement.

SPECIAL SKILLS (optional) (computer lab, foreign language skills, etc.)

REFERENCES (may list names, addresses, and phone numbers of 2–3 references or may indicate, "Available upon Request")

Pratap Gupta

Temporary Address	**Permanent Address**
P.O. Box 3462	1406 Claremont Avenue
Boston, MA 02128	Northbrook, IL 60062
617–555–0000	708–555–2000

OBJECTIVE: A position in a sales training program with the opportunity to advance into management.

EDUCATION **Queens College, Boston, MA**
Bachelor of Arts—English, June 1996
GPA: 3.2
Study Abroad Program in Seville, Spain, Spring Semester, 1994

RELEVANT COURSES: Business Writing, Public Speaking; Business and Organizational Communications; Computer Programming; Accounting; Micro-Economics; Conversational Spanish

EXPERIENCE: **QUEENS PHONATHON, Queens College Development Office, Boston, MA**
Supervisor, September 1995—present
- Motivate, support and encourage 100 student callers in alumni phone solicitation raising over $1,000,000.
- Promoted from fund-raiser.
- Team leader for staff activities.
- Interviewed prospective supervisors and callers for employment and assisted with training.
- Tracked 4 campaigns: Arts & Sciences, MBA, Health Affairs and 40th Reunion.

Fund-raiser, October 1994—April 1995
- Raised over $2,000 personally for the University.
- Used sales and communication skills to raise funds for the University.
- Served as liaison between the University and alumni.

ARTECH CORPORATION, Princeton, NJ
Marketing Assistant, July—September 1995
- Assisted National Training Manager with sales training presentations.
- Used Harvard Graphics and Lotus 1–2–3 extensively.
- Assisted Product Managers with new product information.
- Prepared catalog of training and sales materials.

QUEENS STUDENT CREDIT UNION
Marketing Division Committee, September 1994—May 1995
- Developed marketing strategies targeted toward sophomore and junior classes.

DUPLEX PRODUCTS, INC., Chicago, IL
Sales Representative, May—September 1994
- Coordinated and processed sales orders and purchases of business forms.
- Utilized IBM-PC and mainframe software.
- Made cold calls using telemarketing strategies.
- Wrote sales letters to prospective clients.

QUEENS COLLEGE MARKETING ASSOCIATION, Boston, MA
Publicity Committee, Fall 1993
- Increased student awareness of Marketing Association by developing and posting announcements on campus.
- Invited guest lecturers to speak at meetings.
- Coordinated programs to expose members to career options.

OTHER EXPERIENCE: Sales Associate, Marshall Fields, Oakbrook, IL
Waiter, The Rathskeller, Boston, MA

ACTIVITIES: **Beta Theta Pi Fraternity,** Social Chairman, Songleader
Senator, Morrison Residence Hall
Queens Glee Club

SKILLS:
- Proficient with MS-DOS
- Experienced with many PC software packages including Excel, LOTUS 1–2–3, Harvard Graphics, MS Word, Systat
- Fluent in Spanish

REFERENCES AVAILABLE UPON REQUEST

Valerie Walker
vaw@unc.edu

School Address:
8E City Apartments
425 Vassar Street
Chapel Hill, NC 27514
(919) 555–4567

Home Address:
3901 Cameron Court
Atlanta, GA
(404) 555–4321

OBJECTIVE: Position related to my education and training in Computer Science

RELATED SKILLS:
- Knowledge of IBM PC, Macintosh, DOS, UNIX, OS/S, Windows, Pascal, Basic, C, C++, and NetBIOS.
- Familiarity with debuggers (Codeview, Borland) and word processing, database management, and graphics packages.
- Type approximately 60 wpm.
- Moderate fluency in Spanish.

EDUCATION
University of North Carolina at Chapel Hill.
B.S. Mathematical Sciences—Computer Science Option, May 1996   G.P.A.—3.4
Phi Eta Sigma (Freshman Honor Society)
Dean's List, two semesters

RELEVANT COURSE WORK:
- Distributed Systems
- Operating Systems
- Data Structures
- Computer Organization
- Intermediate Programming I and II
- Introduction to Programming
- Statistical Methods
- Basic Electricity and Magnetism
- Electromagnetism and Optics
- Mechanics (Physics)
- Software Engineering Lab
- Computer Graphics

RELEVANT EXPERIENCE:

Intern, Orange Software, Atlanta, GA, Summer 1995
Developed an upload/download utility for OS/2 StarLAN Toolkit. Program was written in C using NetBIOS interface and supported multiple simultaneous uploads and group downloads. Also responsible for administration of local area network for OS/2 Communications Group.

Intern, Global Information Systems, Columbia, SC Summer 1994
Developed Reference Test System for interoperability of GIS System Network Architecture (SNA) LU6.2 subsystems.

Computer Manager, Carmichael Residence Hall, UNC—Chapel Hill, NC, January–May 1996
Oversaw maintenance of computer equipment and assisted students using computers.

Temporary worker, Hospital Corporation of America, Raleigh, NC, Summer 1993
Developed customized file formatter (Turbo Pascal). Used Symphony word processor and database in support of office procedures. General clerical duties.

ACTIVITIES/ INTERESTS:
Big Buddy program; computer games; magic; juggling; basketball

REFERENCES AVAILABLE UPON REQUEST

SENIOR JOB SEARCH PLAN WORKSHEET

···

August–September

- Draft résumé by (date) _____
- Have critiqued by career office by _____
- Have copies printed by _____
- Register and attend career office orientation by _____
- Attend career office interviewing and job-seeking workshops by _____

- List of possible useful contacts (to be added to as additional ones become known)

  _____

  _____

  _____

  _____

- Other activities:

  _____

  _____

  _____

September–November

- Meet with campus counselor by _____
- Schedule videotaped practice interview with career office by _____

- Check list of campus recruiters and attempt to schedule interviews with _____

  _____

  _____

- Research employers before interviewing.

continued

- Write follow-up letters to the following employers:
  Interviewed with _____ on _____; send follow-up by _____

  _____

  _____

  _____

  _____

  _____

- Attend career fair(s) on _____

- Attend career panels/programs on _____

  _____

December–January (Holiday Break)

- List employers (who are not scheduled to recruit on campus) whom I want to contact:
  Contact _____ by _____

  _____

  _____

  _____

  _____

  _____

- List networking contacts to write or call:
  Contact _____ by _____

  _____

  _____

  _____

  _____

  _____

- Second interviews with the following employers (must be scheduled by employer):

  _____

  _____

  _____

continued

Mid-January–March

- Schedule visit with campus career counselor to discuss progress by
  _____

- On-campus interviews to attempt to obtain and schedule:
  _____
  _____
  _____
  _____

- Follow-up with employers from campus interviews and other contacts:
  Contact _____ by _____
  _____
  _____
  _____
  _____

Mid-March

- Second interview with:
  _____
  _____
  _____

- Attempt to schedule interviews with employers not recruiting on campus:
  Contact _____ by _____
  _____
  _____
  _____

- Call new and previous networking contacts to keep in touch:
  Contact _____ by _____
  _____
  _____
  _____

continued

- Other methods of job seeking (Internet listings, classified ads, professional journals, etc.):

  _____

  _____

  _____

April–May
- Schedule visit with career counselor to discuss progress by _____
- Continue to contact employers of interest:
  Contact _____ by _____

  _____

  _____

  _____

  _____

- Continue to network with contacts:
  Contact _____ by _____

  _____

  _____

  _____

  _____

- Make appointment to discuss job offers (if any) with career counselor by _____

June—Acceptable Job Offer:
- Ensure résumés and contact information are on file with career office before leaving campus.
- Continue employer and network contact:
  Contact _____ by _____

  _____

  _____

  _____

  _____

continued

• Other avenues of job-seeking (classified ads, professional journals, Internet, etc.):

_____

_____

_____

QUESTIONS FREQUENTLY ASKED IN AN INTERVIEW

1. Why did you choose this college/university? Why your particular major?

2. What are your short-term and long-term career goals?

3. Which courses and professors have you enjoyed the most? Why?

4. What do you expect to be doing five years from now?

5. Tell me about yourself.

6. What percentage of your college expenses have you financed yourself?

7. Give me an example of a crisis situation and how you dealt with it.

8. Give me an example of a time you used your leadership skills. What was the outcome?

9. What has been your greatest challenge thus far? How have you attempted to meet that challenge?

10. Give me an example of a time when you failed. What did you learn from the experience?

11. What are your strengths? Your weaknesses?

12. Why are you interested in my organization? Why this position?

13. What do you know about my organization?

continued

14. Give me an example of a situation in which you had to manage time effectively (or set priorities).

15. How do you handle rejection? Criticism?

16. Tell me about a situation when you had to be a good team player. Explain your role on the team.

17. Which organizations have you participated in? What have you learned from your involvement?

18. What have you learned from some of the jobs you've had? Under which type of supervisor do you work best?

19. What are your plans for graduate study?

20. What are your geographic preferences or limitations? Are you willing to travel?

21. What two or three things are most important to you to have in your job?

22. Which criteria will you use to evaluate the organizations with whom you are interviewing?

23. How would your friends describe you?

24. What salary do you expect to receive?

25. Why have you chosen this particular career field?

26. With which other organizations are you interviewing?

27. What questions do you have for me to answer?

28. Tell me about a difficult goal you have set for yourself.

Summary

Basic Tools of the Job Search

The Resume

- Develop a draft based on recommended guidelines
- Have draft critiqued by career office adviser

- Have copies professionally printed on good-quality paper

The Cover Letter

- Use recommended format
- Address the letter to a specific person
- Tailor letter to each organization
- Emphasize the contribution that can be made to the employer
- Use active approach in closing

The Interview

- Prepare thoroughly by researching the organization
- Prepare good questions in advance
- Schedule a videotaped practice interview with a career counselor
- Dress properly for the interview
- Show energy and enthusiasm in the interview
- Attend to both verbal and nonverbal behavior
- Always follow up promptly after the interview

Networking

- Develop and use contacts
- Do not limit contacts to immediate circle
- Send a typed thank-you letter to each contact used

Developing a Strategy

- Determine priorities
- Remain flexible
- Develop a plan and timetable for job search activities
- Do something each week on the job search
- Use as many resources as possible

Parental Support

- Have realistic expectations
- Show an interest in your child's job search
- Give encouragement and support
- Help keep motivation up
- Set guidelines and limits for financial support
- Establish ground rules for adult children returning home

Conversation Starters for Parents and Students

1. What are your major priorities for your first job after college?

2. What type of timetable do you think will work best for you for your job search? Have you worked on a detailed job search plan?

3. Have you started working on your résumé? I'd like to work on it with you. Have you shown it to a counselor at your career office? What suggestions did they make for improvement?

4. Have you drafted a basic cover letter? Has your career office reviewed it and made any suggestions for changes?

5. What kinds of questions are you anticipating from employers who will be interviewing you? Which questions have you prepared to ask them?

6. Have you checked with your career office to see if they offer videotaped practice interviews? Would you like me to role-play an interview with you (or have you role-played an interview with a friend)?

7. Shall we brainstorm together about our possible contacts who may be helpful with your job search?

CHAPTER 9

MAKING THE MOST OF THE COLLEGE CAREER OFFICE

Making allowances for exaggeration, one could say that many college seniors approach their career office as they would a fast-food restaurant: "I'll have one of those biggie jobs with a large order of benefits and some perks on the side." They expect to wait about five minutes (certainly no more than five days) for their order to be filled. Students—as well as parents—can be quite unrealistic about the role of the career office in the job search process.

What responsibility does the career office have to help your child find a job?

The vast majority of college career offices view their role as primarily an educational one. They do not consider themselves employment agencies; in fact, many have taken the word "placement" out of their office name, feeling it gives students the impression that the office will secure a job for them.

The mission statement of the career office of the University of North Carolina at Chapel Hill is fairly typical: "The mission of University Career Services is to provide progressive services and resources that help students prepare for their careers, learn job skills, and find employment." Note the emphasis on providing *services* and *resources* and on *helping* students find employment, rather than finding it for them.

Most career offices are staffed by dedicated, competent career counselors and advisers who are well trained and knowledgeable. They generally have advanced degrees and experience outside an educational setting. They can be very helpful to your son or daughter in every stage of the job search. However, they are not magicians. It is not possible for them to wave a magic wand over the résumé of a senior with a low GPA and three years of experience as a lifeguard, waitress, and sales clerk and create a résumé that will dazzle employers and result in several job offers!

The career office attempts to help underclassmen understand the need for early career planning. In addition to educating students about how to research and plan for their career, the office teaches job search skills and provides linkages with employers.

Career offices advertise their services through various means: the school newspaper, fliers and posters, newsletters, perhaps a home page on the World Wide Web, and possibly even individual letters to you or your student. However, unless your child is enrolled at a very small school, the career office is not likely to have the resources to personally seek out your son or daughter and ask why he or she has not yet used the career office.

It is your child's responsibility to take advantage of the many programs and services offered and to use them well before the senior year. Students who do no preparation for their career and wait until the last possible moment to seek assistance from the career office cannot expect miracles—nor can their parents. Some students do not even visit the career office until after graduation, when they are suddenly panic-stricken. Of course, by then all of the recruiters who were interviewing on campus have long since come and gone, and the jobs they were offering have been filled by students who began interviewing as early as September or October of their senior year. The University of Nebraska at Lincoln posts a sign that reads, "Coming to Career Services after graduation is like studying for finals after the exam!"

When to Go

Students should begin using their college career office no later than their sophomore year. Ideally they will visit the office on a regular basis, getting to know at least one or two of the career advisers and, equally important, ensuring that these advisers know them. Even at very large institutions, it is possible for your son or daughter to develop a close relationship with some of the professional staff to be remembered by them from one visit to the next. If your child is known by the staff, he or she is more likely to be referred when the office receives a job opening that is a perfect match or when an employer asks for the recommendation of a few qualified students.

Occasionally the career office seeks students for unique or one-time opportunities, such as helping an employer with a presentation, or conducting student or employer surveys. The office is likely to call upon students they know for these opportunities, which can develop into valuable contacts and job leads.

Lee was a sophomore interested in exploring career counseling as a career. He volunteered with his campus career office to do any work needed—clerical, computer data entry, library assistance—whatever. After a few months he was appointed to the career services' advisory board, which included students, faculty, and employers.

He also was asked to help with career panels, hosting employer speakers.

Through his work in the career office, he had many conversations with the staff about career options; he eventually decided to combine his interest in career counseling with an interest in business and seek a career in human resources.

Utilizing an employer contact from the career office advisory board, Lee obtained an internship in human resources with a small company for the summer following his sophomore year. That internship, along with school activities the following year, led to another internship the next summer, this time with a large organization. As a senior Lee had strong credentials (not to mention strong advocates at the career office!), which led to several job offers in his chosen field.

When senior year arrives, encourage your child to meet with a career counselor soon after returning to campus in the fall and to continue meeting regularly with the counselor throughout the year. Students planning to graduate in December should begin using the career office for employment assistance two semesters before graduation. Both underclassmen and seniors should use the many programs and services offered through the career office discussed later in this chapter.

In order to be effectively served by the career office, students must follow through on their responsibilities, such as registering for services in a timely manner (usually required for internship assistance, on-campus interviewing, and résumé mailing), providing the office with a sufficient supply of résumés, and checking with the office to ensure that their letters of reference have arrived.

Whom to See and What to Ask

Many career offices have "walk-in" or "drop-in" hours, generally intended for quick questions; students may be limited to a short period of the counselor's time during the walk-in period. Walk-ins are best used for a final review of a résumé or cover letter or for questions that can be easily and quickly answered, such as about the salary range of a given occupation or proper dress for an employer reception.

For anything other than a quick question, it is better for students to schedule an appointment in advance to be assured of meeting with the right staff member for their needs and of having adequate time to discuss their situation.

Many career offices assign professional staff to particular levels of students (such as underclassmen, seniors) or to specialty areas (such as liberal arts or engineering). When visiting the career office, students should explain the reason for their visit to the receptionist and ask which staff member might be best to see.

Your son or daughter will get more out of the visit and reduce the chances of being told to come back to see a different staff member ("who is more knowledgeable about internships," etc.) if he or she is as specific as possible when making the appointment. Your child might say, "I'm a sophomore thinking about a career in computer graphics, and I'd like to talk with someone who can help me prepare for a career in this field," or, "I am a junior business major and would like to schedule an appointment with a counselor who can help me search for a summer internship related to finance."

You may have a son who, like many students, avoids visiting the career office because he is so unsure of a career choice that he does not even know what to ask and is concerned about looking foolish. You can help allay these fears by explaining that the career office exists to help students at all levels of career preparation. Although on some campuses it may be the function of the counseling center rather than the career office to work with unfocused students, all campuses provide assistance with career choice: it is just a matter of finding the correct office, and the career office is usually a good starting point. He should simply state the truth: "I'm clueless about choosing a career."

Or, perhaps you have a daughter who is at the other extreme: she may be so certain of her goal ("I'm going to medical school.") that she assumes that as long as she is taking the necessary courses and doing well academically, there is no need to talk with a career counselor. Most of the time, however, a counselor can provide information that will be helpful, perhaps even critical, for meeting that goal. For example, the counselor might explain that paid or volunteer experience in the health field is virtually a necessity for consideration by medical schools. Additionally, since students' plans often change either by choice or necessity, a counselor can discuss how and why your daughter should develop a backup plan.

Most students are actually somewhere in the middle of the spectrum of deciding on a career; these students often wait to visit the career office until they have a specific reason, such as seeking an internship. This is fine if the reason arises early in the student's college years, but a student who feels there is no need to use the career office until late in senior year could miss out on much-needed information and help.

Five Myths about Career Offices

1. **Myth**—The career office is only helpful for (business, engineering, computer science, etc.) majors.

Fact—The career office can help all majors, although it cannot always provide the same services to all. Campus recruiting, for example, is primarily a function of employer demand rather than career office effort or preference. If your child is interested in a career in broadcasting, for example, chances are high that there will be few, if any, campus interview opportunities, simply because the broadcasting industry does not typically conduct campus recruiting.

Nevertheless, many broadcasting stations list job openings with career offices, so a résumé may be sent by the career office in response to these listings. There are many other ways the career office can help all students, regardless of their major or career interest, such as helping them prepare to be a strong candidate for their chosen field, teaching them job search skills, and providing directories and databases of potential employers and alumni contacts.

2. **Myth**—The career office is for seniors.

Fact—This book has emphasized the need for students to visit their career office by their sophomore year. Virtually all career offices provide individual career counseling, career planning workshops, internship assistance, and career fairs and programs—all services for underclassmen.

3. **Myth**—Many employers who conduct campus interviews are not really hiring.

Fact—Campus interviewing is very expensive for employers. Organizations are not willing to spend time and money on transportation, hotel and meal costs, and lost work time just for public relations purposes. Employers who are interviewing almost always intend to hire, although in some cases they are not sure of the exact number or location of the jobs that will be available upon graduation. This is particularly true for large organizations, which can predict that they will have sales openings, for example, but cannot predict in October or January specifically where the openings will be in May or June.

Although employers visiting a particular campus do intend to consider students from that campus for positions (otherwise they would not be recruiting there), some employers are extremely selective; they may interview as many as 500 students for 10 or 12 openings, resulting in their not making a job offer to any student from some of the campuses they visit.

4. **Myth**—Employers interviewing on campus only hire students with at least a 3.0 GPA.

Fact—Some organizations *do* use a GPA cutoff—in fact some, like investment banks or prestigious technical companies, have a cutoff much higher than a 3.0. Most organizations, however, consider a student's overall background, including work experience, extracurricular activities, and demonstrated leadership skills. Some employers stress these factors much more than grades. Your son or daughter should discuss his or her strengths and interests with a career counselor in order to best determine which employers and industries to target.

5. **Myth**—Very few students get a job through career services.

Fact—What constitutes "getting a job?" Most career offices offer many services and provide assistance in many different ways, all serving to enhance the student's job-seeking skills. This can include a great deal of indirect help, such as critiquing résumés or practice interviews, that eventually pays off. The career office may sponsor a career fair at which a student makes a contact eventually resulting in a job offer; or a career counselor may provide the student with the name of an alumnus working in the student's desired career field, which may prove to be a successful job lead.

Effectively Using Career Office Programs and Services

Although there is some consistency among programs and services offered by career offices, there are also a great many differences: offices vary tremendously in terms of staff size, staff–student ratio, budgets, facilities, philosophy, automation, innovation, and other characteristics. Listed below are programs and services that exist at some, but not necessarily all, career offices. You and your son or daughter may want to call or visit the career office during freshman or sophomore year to inquire about the services offered. (Some prospective college students and parents are even investigating the services of the career office prior to selecting a college.)

Career counseling—As has been previously mentioned, your child should meet periodically with the career adviser for his or her major or interest area. Students often wrongly assume that counselors are too busy to see them (especially on large campuses) and never check, losing out on the opportunity available for individual help. They miss out on the chance for expert advice at no charge. Many, upon graduating without a job or direction, realize they need professional help and may then have to pay as much as $75–100 an hour for private career counseling.

Interest testing and computerized guidance progams—Most campuses offer career guidance for undecided students. Assistance may be through counseling, interest testing, and—an increasingly popular option— computerized programs. These services may be provided by the career office or the counseling center, depending on the particular college or university. If your son or daughter is unsure of a major or career choice, he or she should inquire at the career office about available help.

Career fairs and programs—Your child should check with the career office in August or September to obtain its schedule of programs for the year or at least for the fall semester. (Most career offices plan far in advance.) He or she should mark these programs on the calendar so as not to forget them. Career fairs, career panels, and other career programs are important ways for students to learn about occupations and how to prepare for them and to make valuable contacts. Students should participate in these programs each year, starting as a freshman or sophomore.

Career planning and job search workshops—Most career offices offer workshops on such topics as planning for a career, obtaining an internship, résumé writing, interviewing, and job search strategies. Some offices have workshops on specialized topics, such as business etiquette, networking, and employment trends. Encourage your child to attend as many workshops as possible. These are valuable services that may prove costly if your child is interested in them following graduation.

Career planning course (for academic credit)—Many colleges and universities offer a career planning course for credit, often taught by staff of the career office. Such a course is especially useful for undecided students but can be helpful for all students. Since students often put off planning for their career and doing the requisite research and activities, a course can help ensure that these activities get done.

Cooperative education and internship assistance—Almost all schools provide help to students desiring internships, and many have co-op programs. Your son or daughter should check with the career office early in the fall of sophomore and junior years to learn about the services available for experiential learning (co-op and internship experiences). Again, students cannot expect to be placed in a co-op or internship by the career office, but they should receive help conducting a campaign to search for the position (including help with writing a résumé, interview tips, directories of employers, position listings, etc.). Many career offices have campus interviews and a résumé-referral service for co-op and internship positions.

Externships/Job-shadowing programs—Students may have the opportunity through their career office to have a short-term experience observing someone doing the type of work in which they are interested. Externships, sometimes called job-shadowing programs, generally take place over fall or spring break or at another time when students are free from class. (Some schools, such as Dartmouth College, have a three-week free period in January—"the Jan term"—during which students often participate in externships.)

Resource room/Career and employer library—All career offices have a resource room, or career library, although some will be more extensive than others. In the career library your son or daughter will find information about many occupations, employers, and job search skills. An increasing number of career offices now have many of these resources available on computer. Some career offices have their library staffed with an employee or student helper, but many are designed for self-help. If your child is confused by the organization of the library or cannot find the necessary information, by all means have him or her ask for assistance. Unfortunately, many students become discouraged when they cannot find the resource they need, and leave without requesting help.

Alumni databases—Students can usually obtain contact information for alumni working in various fields through their career office. Many offices have such data in an automated database, making it easy for students to search by various criteria, such as "alumni/ae working in publishing in Boston." These alumni have volunteered to help students and are eager to be contacted, yet students sometimes complain that they write to alumni and do not hear back from them. It is suggested that students call alumni in order to make it as easy as possible for them to respond.

Practice (mock) interviews—If the career office offers the opportunity for students to have a mock, or practice, interview, your child should schedule one. Many offices have the capability to videotape the practice interview. This service is one of the most valuable learning experiences for job hunters, yet it is widely underused. Perhaps students are embarrassed to have their mistakes captured on video or they are simply unaware of the service; in any case, those students who do take advantage of this service consistently rate it as highly valuable. It is far better for a student to look foolish in a practice interview with a counselor than in a real interview for a job!

Campus interviews—Students and their parents often focus almost exclusively on the number and type of employers interviewing on campus. Campus interviewing is certainly convenient for students and is productive, if only because it gives them an opportunity to hone their interviewing skills; however, most students will not obtain a job through this method. Many industries do not conduct any campus interviews; and hiring for many jobs, such as public relations or nonprofit work, is rarely done through campus recruiting.

Students should view campus interviewing as one of the many services provided by the career office that can help them in their job search. (Occasionally there are campus interviews for cooperative education or internship positions as well.) They should not look at campus interviews as an all-or-nothing situation: That is, they should not put all of their eggs in this one basket, expecting to find a job through campus interviews and doing nothing additional in their job search. But neither should they summarily dismiss campus interviews as having nothing for them! Encourage your son or daughter to register with the career office in order to be eligible to interview and to regularly check the schedule of employers visiting campus. They may be quite pleasantly surprised to see employers as diverse as Liz Claiborne, J. P. Morgan, Teach for America, Target, IBM, and the NBA recruiting on their campus. The number and type of employers recruiting will greatly depend on the job market as well as the size of the college or university, its reputation among employers, and its production of graduates with the academic preparation and other qualifications sought by employers.

Career offices use various methods for student interview sign-up. Because there may be more students interested in interviewing with an employer than there are interview slots available, career offices may have the employer select the students to be interviewed (generally from résumés submitted by students in advance of the employer visit), or the career office may select the candidates from a bidding, lottery, or other system. If your son or daughter is having difficulty obtaining interviews with desired employers, he or she should discuss this with a counselor. There are often ways around "the system," such as writing directly to the employer and requesting consideration, or attaching a compelling letter to the résumé that the career office sends to the employer.

Video interviewing—A new service available on some campuses is video interviewing, which allows students to be interviewed by employers at a remote location via a computer and video equipment. While video interviewing is not quite the same as an in-person interview, it is far ahead of a telephone interview, since it allows greater interaction between both parties. This technology is new and not yet widely used; however, for campuses on which it is available, it expands opportunities for students to interact with employers who are not visiting campus.

Employer databases—Many career office libraries, especially on large campuses, have employer information available on computer, sometimes on CD-ROM. One employer database, Career Search, contains information on over 400,000 employers, which can be searched by such characteristics as industry, location, or size of employer. These databases do not have job openings (much to students' dismay), but they are extremely useful for developing lists of employers to target and for obtaining brief employer profiles.

Résumé-mailing service—On most campuses the number of employers conducting recruiting visits is decreasing, whereas the number of employers listing job openings is increasing. Many employers, particularly small ones, do not have the budget or staff available for campus recruiting; additionally, they may have a need for only one or two employees and may need these employees immediately. These employers will often contact the career office and request the office to send them résumés of qualified students. Some large career offices may receive as many as 2,000 or more job requests a year.

It is definitely to your child's advantage to inquire about this service and the requirements for participation. Generally a student will need to register with the career office and have a résumé (or several copies) on file. Often students do not realize that the majority of résumé-referral activity takes place in late spring or summer, just before or after graduation. They may deposit résumés with the career office early in their senior year and become discouraged if they are not contacted by employers. However, if students are graduating without a job, it is important to stay in touch with the career office, letting the office know that they wish to be referred for any positions that might relate to their interests. They must check periodically with the career office to be sure that the office has a sufficient supply of their résumés on file.

Reference-mailing service—Fewer and fewer career offices maintain reference files for all students because many employers wish to directly contact references rather than receive a copy of a written letter on file with the career office. Nevertheless, this service is available on some campuses for either all students or for those with specialized needs, like students applying to graduate or professional school or students in particular majors, such as education or health sciences. This service is convenient for students, since it allows them to have their letters of reference on file at the career office. They can then request that the letters be mailed by the office each time they apply to a graduate or professional school. The reference mailing service eliminates the need to contact their references each time they need a letter and ensures that the letters will be sent in a timely manner. There is typically a fee to establish a reference file and an additional fee for each mailing. Your son or daughter should ask if this service is available.

WWW home page—An increasing number of career offices have established a home page on the World Wide Web. The home page allows students seven-day-a-week, 24-hour access to much of the career office information such as job listings, recruiting schedule, or list of services. The career office home page also links to other job search resources available on the Internet.

Job hot line and job listings—All career offices maintain job listings. These listings may include permanent, summer, part-time, internship, and cooperative education positions. Distribution and posting of the jobs varies widely: some offices list the positions in binders or file folders; others produce a job-listing newsletter, which they post or mail to students and alumni; and others post job listings electronically, perhaps on a home page, on an automated telephone job hot line, or in a computer database. Your child should find out how the campus career office posts job openings and should check the openings frequently.

Graduate and professional school advising—This service may be a function of the career office on some campuses, whereas on others it is handled by another department, possibly in the graduate school or the office of academic advising. If your child has an interest in further education, he or she should find out which office handles advising and begin talking with a graduate school adviser by sophomore year or as soon as his or her interest develops.

Graduate and professional school fairs and forums—Many career offices also sponsor graduate and professional school fairs and forums. These are programs attended by admissions representatives from many educational institutions. The programs may be dedicated to one professional specialty, such as law or business schools, or may be of a general nature, with representatives from many graduate schools across the country. Students should not wait until their senior year to attend these programs, since the information they glean from the representatives can be invaluable for preparing adequately for admission. The admissions representatives can provide information on desired major, work experience, course work, grades, and other qualities needed to be a competitive candidate for acceptance to their school. If your child has even the slightest interest in graduate or professional school, he or she should ask the career office about these programs.

Follow-up surveys and statistics—It is helpful for your son or daughter to know what graduates of his or her school and major have done after graduation and how they found their jobs. The career office should be able to provide this data from surveys, often called follow-up surveys. Of course, statistics can never predict what will happen to any one individual—your child may be the one journalism major who is hired directly out of school by the *Wall Street Journal* at a starting salary of $36,000; however, statistics can help to realistically set expectations about salary, length of time to find a job, type of employment, and sources leading to employment in a particular field. Do not wait until the senior year to request this information from the career office; it can be a valuable resource for making academic and career decisions throughout college.

Alumni services—Most career offices provide services to graduates for at least six months after graduation without charge. Beyond that, offices vary in terms of the length of time a graduate may use the office and the fees (if any) charged; some career offices allow alumni to use their services indefinitely, whereas others have a cutoff point of one to five years after graduation. The university alumni office will generally offer career assistance to graduates who are no longer eligible to use the career office.

Conclusion

If used early, effectively, and often, the career office can be extremely helpful to your son or daughter in the job search. Most offices are happy to answer questions from interested and concerned parents. Remember, though, that your child must take responsibility for planning a career and for putting forth the effort that it takes to find a job in today's competitive environment. Neither you nor the career office can or should do that; but with your support, the career office's assistance, and your son or daughter's commitment, your child should be able to attain his or her career goal.

Summary

Realistic Expectations of the Career Office

The career office:

- Can provide services and resources to help students

- Can provide individual assistance to students

- Is not responsible for finding a job for students

When to Go

Students should:

- Visit the career office by their sophomore year

- Use the career office frequently

- Begin using the career office two semesters before graduation for employment assistance

Whom to See/What to Ask

Students should:

- Be as specific as possible about their needs when making an appointment

- Request to see the counselor for their major or career interests

- Be candid with the career counselor about their needs

Five Myths about Career Offices

- The career office is only helpful for certain majors

- The career office is only for seniors

- Many employers interviewing on campus are not hiring

- Employers interviewing on campus require a 3.0 GPA

- Very few students get a job through career services

Career Office Programs and Services That May Be Available

- Individual career counseling

- Interest testing and computerized career guidance programs

- Career fairs and programs

- Career planning and job search workshops

- Career planning course for credit

- Cooperative education and internship assistance

- Externship/job-shadowing programs
- Resource room/career and employer library
- Alumni databases
- Practice (mock) interviews
- Campus interviews
- Video interviewing
- Employer databases
- Résumé-mailing service
- Reference-mailing service
- WWW home page
- Job hot line and job listings
- Graduate/professional school advising
- Graduate/professional school fairs and forums
- Follow-up surveys/statistics
- Alumni services

Conversation Starters for Parents and Students

1. Have you checked with the career office to learn about the services they offer for underclassmen? For seniors? Please tell me about these services.

2. Which of the services and programs of the career office do you think will be most useful to you? Why?

3. Which employers are coming to campus to interview this year? With whom would you like to interview?

4. Have you looked at the follow-up surveys of past graduates? What types of jobs have other graduates in your field found, and what were the typical salaries? Which methods did they state were most useful to them in their job search?

5. Who is the career counselor for your major or career interests? Have you met with him or her? What advice did he or she provide? Are you regularly using this counselor as a resource for your questions about your career planning and job search?

CAMPUS RESOURCES FOR FURTHER INFORMATION

Contact	Appropriate Topics
Office of Career Services (cooperative education or internships may be administered in another office)	Career choice, career planning; internships, cooperative education, short-term job options; job search skills and activities, job listings, occupational and employer information, employment statistics on graduates; graduate/professional school advice
University Counseling Center (may be combined with Career Services)	Personal problems; career choice (interest and personality testing; computerized guidance programs; vocational counseling); selecting a major; test anxiety; study skills
Student Activities Coordinator	List of campus clubs/organizations; other opportunities for leadership training and development
Learning Center (may have other names such as Reading Center, or Academic Support Center)	Tutoring; study skills; preparation for graduate/professional school admission tests
Student's Academic Adviser	Your child's academic progress relative to other students; academic difficulties; university academic requirements for major, for graduation, and for department honors
Academic Dean	Questions/problems relating to admission to a specific academic program

continued

Study-Abroad Office	Study-abroad/exchange programs, including whether credits are accepted, costs; internships abroad
Financial Aid/Work-Study Office	Financial aid qualifications; work-study programs; scholarships (academic as well as need-based)
Faculty Members	Course questions, waiver of prerequisites for course admission; opportunities to work as a grader, teaching assistant, or research assistant.
Registrar's Office	Transcript requests/questions; requirements for Dean's List, Phi Beta Kappa, other honors
University's Graduate/Professional School Adviser	Graduate/professional school preparation, application (including admission test dates); impact of graduating early or late on graduate/professional school admission

APPENDIX: RECOMMENDED RESOURCES AND ADDITIONAL INFORMATION

CAREER PLANNING

Carney, Clarke G., and Linda Field Wells. *Discover the Career within You* (Pacific Grove, Calif.: Brooks/Cole Publishing, 1995).

Fischer, Carolyn A., and Carol A. Schwartz, Editors. *Encyclopedia of Associations* (Detroit, MI: Gale Research, Inc., 1996).

Phifer, Paul. *Career Planning Q's and A's* (Garrett Park, Md.: Garrett Park Press, 1990).

Powell, C. Randall. *Career Planning Today* (Dubuque, Iowa: Kendall/Hunt Publishing, 1990).

Schrank, Louise Walsh. *How to Choose the Right Career* (Lincolnwood, Ill.: NTC Publishing Group, 1991).

Stoodley, Martha. *Information Interviewing* (Garret Park, Md.: Garrett Park Press, 1990).

Tener, Elizabeth. *The Smith College Job Guide* (New York: Penguin Books USA, 1991).

CAREER CHOICE

The Encyclopedia of Career Choices for the 90's (New York: The Putnam Publishing Group, 1992).

Field, Shelby. *100 Best Careers for the Year 2000* (New York: Prentice Hall, 1992).

Kleiman, Carol. *The 100 Best Jobs for the 1990's and Beyond* (Chicago: Dearborn Financial Publishing, 1992).

Krannich, Ronald L., and Caryl Rae Krannich. *The Best Jobs for the 1990's and into the 21st Century* (Manassas Park, Va.: Impact Publications, 1995).

Krantz, Les. *The National Business Employment Weekly Jobs Rated Almanac* (New York; John Wiley & Sons, 1995).

Occupational Outlook Handbook (Washington, D.C.: Bureau of Labor Statistics, 1996). Published biannually.

Wright, John, and Edward Dwyer. *The American Almanac of Jobs and Salaries* (New York: Avon Books, 1992).

CHOOSING A MAJOR

Basta, Nicholas. *Major Options* (New York: HarperCollins, 1991).

Carter, Carol. *Majoring in the Rest of Your Life* (New York: Farrar, Straus, and Giroux, 1990).

The College Board Guide to 150 Popular College Majors (New York: College Board Publications, 1992).

Figler, Howard. *Liberal Education and Careers Today* (Garret Park, Md.: Garrett Park Press, 1989).

Nadler, Burton Jay. *Liberal Arts Jobs* (Princeton, N.J.: Peterson's, 1986).

Phifer, Paul. *College Majors and Careers* (Garrett Park, Md.: Garrett Park Press, 1993).

INTERNSHIPS

Cantrel, Will, and Francine Modderno. *International Internships and Volunteer Programs* (Oakton, Va.: WorldWise Books, 1992).

Gilbert, Sara D. *Internships: A Directory for Career-Finders* (New York: Arco Publishing, 1995).

Internships 1996 (Princeton, N.J.: Peterson's 1995).

Job Choices: 1996 in Business (Bethlehem, Penn.: National Association of Colleges and Employers, 1995).

Job Choices: 1996 in Science and Engineering (Bethelehem, Penn.: National Association of Colleges and Employers, 1995).

Martin, Garrett D., and Barbara E. Baker. *The National Directory of Internships* (Raleigh, N.C.: National Society for Experiential Education, 1995).

National Directory of Arts Internships (Los Angeles: National Network for Artist Placement, 1995).

Oldman, Mark, and Samer Hamadeh. *America's Top 100 Internships* (New York: Villard Books, 1995).

————. *The Internship Bible* (New York: Random House, Inc. 1995).

Smithsonian Opportunities for Research and Study in History, Art, and Sciences (Washington, D.C.: Smithsonian Institution, 1995–96).

GRADUATE AND PROFESSIONAL SCHOOL

Bell, Susan J. *Full Disclosure: Do You Really Want to Be a Lawyer?* (Princeton, N.J.: Peterson's, 1992).

Bernal, Deborah L. *Vital Signs: Working Doctors Tell the Real Story Behind Medical School & Practice* (Princeton, N.J.: Peterson's, 1994).

Byrne, John A. *Business Week Guide to the Best Business Schools* (New York: McGraw-Hill, 1995).

Feibelman, Peter J. *A Ph.D. is Not Enough: A Guide to Survival in Science* (Reading, Mass.: Addison-Wesley Publishing, 1993).

Lopos, George J., Margaret E. Holt, Richard E. Bohlander, and John H. Wells, eds. *Guide to Certificate Programs at American Colleges and Universities* (Princeton, N.J.: Peterson's, 1988).

Medical School Admission Requirements, United States and Canada (Washington, D.C.: Association of American Medical Colleges, 1995–96). Published annually.

Peters, Robert L. *Getting What You Came For: The Smart Student's Guide to Earning an MA or Ph.D.* (New York: Noonday Press, 1992).

Peterson's Guide to Graduate and Professional Programs 1996 (Princeton, N.J.: Peterson's, 1995). Published annually.

Peterson's Guide to MBA Programs (Princeton, N.J.: Peterson's, 1995).

Stelzer, Richard J. *How to Write a Winning Personal Statement for Graduate and Professional School* (Princeton, N.J.: Peterson's, 1993).

Swartz, Harold M., and Diane Gottheil, eds. *The Education of Physician Scholars* (Rockville, Md.: Betz Publishing, 1993).

Van Tuyl, Ian. *The Best Law Schools* (New York: Random House, 1995).

Wagner, Andrea. *How to Land Your First Paralegal Job* (Los Angeles: Estrin Publishing, 1992).

TAKING TIME OFF

Alternatives to the Peace Corps: A Directory of Third World & U.S. Volunteer Opportunities (Oakland, Calif.: Food First, 1994).

Council on International Educational Exchange. *Work, Study, Travel Abroad: The Whole World Handbook* (New York: St. Martin's Press, 1996).

International Directory of Volunteer Programs (New York: The Council on International Educational Exchange, 1996).

DuBois, Jennifer, and Mark Conley. *Now Hiring! Destination Resort Jobs* (Seattle, Wash.: Perpetual Press, 1994).

Gilpin, Robert, with Caroline Fitzgibbons. *Time Out: Taking a Break from School to Travel, Work & Study in the U.S. and Abroad* (New York: Simon & Schuster, 1992).

Griffith, Susan. *Teaching English Abroad* (Princeton, N.J.: Peterson's Guides, 1994).

Justice, Peggy O'Connell. *The Temp Track: Make One of the Hottest Job Trends of the 90's Work for You* (Princeton, N.J.: Peterson's, 1993).

Maltzman, Jeffrey. *Jobs in Paradise: The Definitive Guide to Exotic Jobs Everywhere* (New York: Harper & Row, 1993).

McMillon, Bill. *Volunteer Vacations: Short-term Adventures That Will Benefit You and Others* (Chicago: Chicago Review Press, 1995).

Peterson's Study Abroad 1996: Semester, Summer and Year Abroad Academic Programs (Princeton, NJ: Peterson's, 1995).

JOB SEEKING/RESUME WRITING/ INTERVIEWING

Asher, Donald. *The Overnight Resume* (Berkeley, Calif.: Ten Speed Press, 1991).

Bolles, Richard Nelson. *The 1996 What Color Is Your Parachute?* (Berkeley, Calif.: Ten Speed Press, 1996). Revised annually.

Figler, Howard. *The Complete Job Search Handbook* (New York: Henry Holt and Company, 1988).

Frank, William S. *200 Letters for Job Hunters* (Berkeley, Calif.: Ten Speed Press, 1990).

Gonyea, James C. *The On-Line Job Search Companion* (New York: McGraw-Hill, 1995).

Hermann, Richard L., and Linda P. Sutherland. *The 110 Biggest Mistakes Job Hunters Make (And How To Avoid Them)* (Washington, D.C.: Federal Reports, 1992).

Kaplan, Bobbie Miller. *Sure-Hire Cover Letters* (New York: AMACOM, 1994).

Kennedy, Joyce Lain, and Thomas J. Morrow. *Electronic Job Search Revolution* (New York: John Wiley & Sons, 1994).

———. *Electronic Resume Revolution* (New York: John Wiley & Sons, 1994).

Krannich, Ronald L., and William J. Banis. *High Impact Resumes & Cover Letters* (Manassas Park, Va.: IMPACT Publications, 1995).

Medley, H. Anthony. *Sweaty Palms: The Neglected Art of Being Interviewed* (Berkeley, Calif.: Ten Speed Press, 1993).

Nadler, Burton Jay. *Naked at the Interview* (New York: John Wiley & Sons, 1994).

Richardson, Douglas B., *Networking* (New York: John Wiley & Sons, 1994).

Shingleton, John D. *Successful Interviewing for College Seniors* (Lincolnwood, Ill.: NTC Publishing, 1992).

Weddle, Peter D. *Electronic Resumes for the New Job Market* (Manassas Park, Va.: IMPACT Publications, 1995).

Yate, Martin. *Cover Letters That Knock 'Em Dead* (Holbrook, Mass.: Adams Media Corporation, 1995).

Yate, Martin. *Knock 'Em Dead: The Ultimate Job-Seeker's Handbook* (Holbrook, Mass.: Adams Media Corporation, 1995).

BUSINESS ETIQUETTE

Craig, Betty. *Don't Slurp Your Soup* (New Brighton, Minn.: Brighton Publications, 1991).

Fountain, Elizabeth Haas. *The Polished Professional* (Hawthorne, N.J.: Career Press, 1994).

CONTACT INFORMATION

Organization	Telephone Number
American Zionist Youth Foundation	212-339-6916
Camphill Village	518-329-7924
Career Discovery–Harvard University	617-495-5453
Carolina Publishing Institute	800-845-8640
Center for Austrian Studies	612-624-9811
CET-Wellesley College	800-225-4262
CIEE (The Council on International Educational Exchange)	212-661-1414
Columbia Business Careers Institute	212-854-3331
Green Corps	202-597-9178
Habitat for Humanity	912-924-6935
The International Foundation	414-786-6700
Internships in Europe	914-245-6882
Jesuit Volunteer Corps	215-232-0300
JET (Japanese Exchange and Teaching Program)	202-939-7600
Lutheran Volunteer Corps	202-387-3222
McIntire Business Institute (University of Virginia)	804-924-7010

National Institutes of Health	301-496-7735
Peace Corps	800-424-8580
Performance Research	401-848-0111
Princeton in Asia	609-258-3657
Radcliffe Publishing Course	617-495-8678
Sotheby's Educational Studies	212-606-7822
Spoleto Festival	803-722-2764
Teach for America	800-832-1230
Time Magazine	212-522-2388
U.S. Department of Justice	202-307-0567
Volunteers in Asia	415-723-3228
White & Case	212-819-8200
WorldTeach	617-495-5527
Yale China	203-432-0880